Concepts of Coaching

Dedicated to Fiona, Catriona and Murray

Concepts of Coaching

A guide for managers

PETER HILL

Institute of Leadership & Management (ILM)
1 Giltspur Street
London
EC1A 9DD
United Kingdom

Tel: +44 (0)20 7294 8241
Fax: +44 (0)20 7294 2402
E-mail: info@i-l-m.com
Website: http://www.i-l-m.com

First published in Great Britain in 2004

ISBN: 1 902475 23 2

© ILM, 2004

British Library Cataloguing-in-Publication Data.

A catalogue record for this book is available from the British Library.

Book production by Chandos Publishing (Oxford) Limited (*www.chandospublishing.com*)
Typeset by Turn-Around Typesetting, UK
Printed by Chris Fowler International Ltd, London

Contents

Appendices

Acknowledgements

To my wife and coach, Fiona, who supplies a lifetime of inspiration and love in a moment, every moment. To my children, Catriona and Murray, whose childlike innocence, questions and learning journeys have allowed me to revisit childhood and gain an education. To Tony Morgan, who had the knowledge and foresight to see what I couldn't and to have the guts to stand by his word and put it into action. To Myles Downey under whom I couldn't have served a better apprentiship in the field of non-directive coaching. To my past colleagues at the School of Coaching. To Barbara Cohen who first introduced me to mentoring, its benefits and challenges. To Graham Houston whose passion for patriotism matches his passion for people development. To my past colleagues at the Industrial Society in the Glasgow office for all their learning, tutelage and guidance. With special thanks to Louise Beaton and Heather McIntyre who tidied up a lot of the early work and for putting up with me. To the coaches and clients of the coaching project mentioned in the section on evaluation for seeing their delight in proving others wrong and having fun while doing it. Especially to Tony Bolton and his family for the constant support, humour and love despite the ups and downs of the sporting world. A special thanks to Marjory, a great juggling coach. To Ian Chisholm who in the face of all adversity, including moving his family halfway around the world, managed to stay loyal to the cause of coaching and what it stands for. To Anne Marie Daniel for some fantastic cooking on the Isle of Skye as well as some sublime insights into people's behaviour. To Colin Mackenzie for his gentle approach to people development that yields phenomenal results and Anne Welsh for her due diligence. To Mary Musselbrook for her gentle tenacity in the field of appreciative enquiry and her companionship. To Sue Knight for her authenticity. To the numerous authors, coaches and colleagues for treading the path before me and making the journey so much easier. To David Whyte, Sir John Whitmore and Tim Gallwey who deliver with such professional ease, soul and integrity. To Aileen Gibb and her team for building 'a stage for the soul to perform on'. Acknowledgement also goes to the numerous people such as Sally Gough who have been on the receiving end of some very dubious mentoring and have still had the faith in themselves to succeed. For the raw product that is Peter Hill, thanks to my Mum, who sadly never got to see the fruits of my labours, and to my Dad and brother who provided a fantastic backdrop for learning. And finally to Fiona, again, for the hours of copy typing during the production stage.

The above have all been involved, directly or indirectly, in this book and it is all the better for that. Any mistakes, flaws or omissions belong to me and as such provide another opportunity for learning.

Peter Hill

Permissions

The author and publishers wish to thank and acknowledge the following for their generosity in allowing their work to be included in this text.

Page

46   Dr Keith Rogers and Karen Tidswell: 'Practical Learning Styles' – published in 2002.

50   John Heron: 'The Catalytic Toolkit' – published by Sage Publications Ltd in 1998.

93   Sir John Whitmore: 'The GROW Model' – published by Nicholas Brealey Publishing in 2002.

98   Myles Downey: 'The Coaching Spectrum' – published by Texere Publishing, part of Thomson South-Western Professional, in 2003.

107   Max Landsberg: 'The Skill/Will Matrix' – published by Profile Books in 1996.

112   Tim Gallwey: 'The STOP Tool' – published by Texere Publishing, part of Thomson South-Western Professional, in 2000.

133   James Lawley and Penny Tompkins: 'Symbolic Domain and Clean Questions' – published by The Developing Press Company Ltd in 2000.

146   Jon Katzenbach and Douglas Smith: 'Team Basics and Team Performance Curve' – published by Harvard Business School Publishing in 1998.

176–9 Lorna Brown Design Ltd: Figures 5.1 to 5.5.

191   Paul Kearns and Tony Miller: 'The KPMT Model' – published by Pearson Education in 1997.

219   Julie Hay, European Mentoring and Coaching Council: 'The EMCC Code of Ethics' – published by the EMCC in 2004.

227   Barbara Cohen: 'The Ten Core Coaching Competencies' – published by Hyperion/CFM in 2000.

Full acknowledgements can be found at the end of each section. The author believes he has identified all rightful ownership of works included in this text. However, it is possible that some may have been overlooked. If this is the case the author apologies for any inconvenience or embarrassment caused and would request that he be contacted so that any future editions can be corrected to include rightful ownership.

About the author

Peter Hill is a professionally qualified business coach with a reputation for 'getting things done through people'. His determination, drive and sense of humour enable results to be delivered in a way that many people enjoy. His approach is through application and understanding and his learning is through immersion. His ability to marry a logical and practical approach with emotional understanding has led to a previous employer achieving Investors in People status, gaining NEBSM (ILM) recognition and securing certification with the University of Strathclyde for the UK's first School of Coaching.

Peter is currently the Managing Partner with CFM Consulting Ltd and has clients in the public and private sectors in finance, commerce, industry, IT, and voluntary and social services. At present, Peter is working with a number of individual senior clients to assist in their desire to improve their behaviours and performance in the corporate and private arenas. In previous work he has facilitated boards and senior management teams to enable increased understanding of the complex nature of their business. He has assisted in finding ways to harness the best of the various elements that individuals bring to their respective companies, aligning these elements in a way that does not privilege one aspect of the business over another. Peter employs a number of tools and techniques which, while innovative, have a solid practical application in the world of work.

Peter has been involved with ILM since its formation in 2003 and with the National Examinations Board for Supervisory Management since 1990. He was involved in the development of the ILM's Coaching and Mentoring Qualifications and the development of four levels of Qualifications in Coaching through the University of Strathclyde.

Peter left the Industrial Society in 2000 to set up CFM Consulting, a company specialising in coaching and 'enabling people to lead the lives they were born to live'.

The author may be contacted as follows:

Tel: 01786 821272
Mobile: 07802 753545
E-mail: *Peter@cfmconsulting.net*
Website: *www.coachingformore.co.uk*

Introduction

For many years leadership has been the driving force of the world of work. There have been many debates over the differences between managers and leaders, doing the right thing and doing things right and making sure common sense becomes common practice.

The common denominator in these discussions was people – how to get more (output) from less (people), how to motivate them, how to understand them and in many cases how to manipulate them. It is this last aspect that flags up the need for something else.

Coaching has landed on the world of work with immense impact and an amazing variety of approaches.

In this book I have used many of the approaches I have taken with clients and commissioning companies while plying my trade as a professionally qualified coach.

There is a variety of models and concepts – hence the title of the book – and sources of reference to assist you in making your journey into the world of coaching a lot more enjoyable for you and your clients.

I have also added further reading at the end of the sections and chapters that will take your learning to a different plane.

If you can get your coaching right the rewards are immense. I remember working in my father's garage rebuilding engines that had been trashed by their owners and taking great pleasure in stripping them down, cleaning them, rebuilding them and installing them back in their original car. I would always take pride in doing the job properly, giving the keys back to the customer and getting them to start the car for the first time since the rebuild. They always looked surprised when it started first time! For me it was job satisfaction personified. I just didn't think it could get any better until many years later when I coached my first client – the feeling that 'this was what I was put on the planet for' hit me. That feeling has been with me since that very first day and continues to inspire me.

I hope you find some inspiration in this book that will help you to lead the life you were born to live.

The context of coaching

Over the past 10 to 15 years coaching has developed as a profession in its own right. While still very much in its infancy standards are developing further (see Appendix 1) and professional qualifications are on the increase (see pp. 6–9). Certainly it is developing at a rapid pace. According to Zeus and Skiffington in *The Coaching at Work Toolkit* (2003), coaching is second only to the IT industry in terms of growth rate in the United States. With this growth comes subsequent challenges and opportunities that make it such an interesting profession. Coaching itself in today's world of work is a practice – it is not about what you do, it is about how you are. To quote Angeles Arrien's Principles in *The Four-Fold Way* (1993), it is about showing up and choosing to be present. Paying attention. Telling the truth. Being open to outcome, not attached to results. How different this is to the world of work many of us know, understand and live in. It is probably more commonplace than any of us realise. In 1999 a survey of HR professionals found that 90 per cent of companies in the United States offer some form of coaching to their key executives and some of the areas in which coaching was deployed were leadership development, retention of top staff, management succession planning and ensuring success after promotions or new hires. So while the industry has actually grown there is still a lot of opportunity – not mentioned, for example, is the use of coaching as reinforcement for training programmes. However, we know that training has developed over the past twenty years and now has a substantially higher investment rate.

Most of the research that is available today[1] comes from our colleagues across the Atlantic and it was Manchester Consulting Inc. which conducted the first major research project to quantify the business impact of executive coaching. The study consisted of 100 executives who had completed a coaching programme between 1996 and 2000. They found that the estimated return on investment (ROI) was 5.7 times the initial investment outlay. A recent study outlined by Zeus and Skiffington (2002) explored the outcomes of the coaching process from two aspects, the inter-personal and the intra-personal. The executives reported that they had become more aware of themselves and others and as a consequence assumed more responsibility for their actions. There is no doubt that it led to a positive change in performance.

Coaching generally exists on two fronts in the workplace today: large-scale coaching interventions to train managers to act more as coaches thus extending their leadership style, and coaching executives at a more senior level within the organisation. In both cases it is usually a remedial performance coaching model that is actually used, which, as mentioned before, still leaves us with the opportunity to develop things for the future in true proactive coaching style.

Coaching today, as we know it, has many of its principles founded in areas such as counselling and sports psychology. The number of books that actually link sports to business coaching are innumerable (see the Bibliography at the end of the book). While there is no doubt there is a strong relationship between sports coaching and counselling, business coaching itself has a particular slant that needs to be fine-tuned and developed for the appropriate audience. It is not difficult to see why coaching has become so popular. The main driver over the last 25 years in business and industry has been information technology. Back in the 1960s not many organisations had an IT department (and some people may say they were better days!). However, the rise of information technology and the constant drive for better communication has meant that there has been increasing turbulence and massive change in the world of work. The need for leadership has never been greater than it is in the early twenty-first century. Having said that, it will be greater still in the latter part of the century. As a result, leadership and training somehow sold itself short in this area and coaching has found its niche in completing the learning cycle. Follow-up action through training programmes is now quite commonplace with managers taking a coaching approach to brief individuals before they go on and after they complete training programmes. The Manchester Consulting Inc. survey quoted earlier suggested that without follow-on coaching 87 per cent of new skills learned will be lost and given that training costs are getting higher many organisations want to ensure that they get maximum return on investment.

There is one other twist to coaching in the workplace today, once again related to information technology. In today's world e-mails are routine and as such there has been a decline in the accurate and grammatical use of the English language. This has led to a rise in educational books with such wonderful titles as *Eats, Shoots and Leaves* (Truss, 2004), *Tales for Coaching* (Parkin, 2001) and *Tales for Trainers* (Parkin, 1998). This is not good news for the coach in one respect as language is the only tool that the coach has. However, it is good news given the opportunity that it now presents the coach within the world of work. Certainly my first introduction to coaching was brought about through Tony Morgan and his associates and colleagues such as Sir John Whitmore, Miki Wallaczek and Lewis Maciver, all of whom use distinction-based learning to make significant breakthroughs in the world of work. Tony latterly introduced me and many others in the Industrial Society, where he was the Chief Executive, to David Whyte who takes this to a completely new dimension by using poetry as the vehicle for driving breakthroughs into the workplace. David and his colleagues such as John

O'Donohue have developed wonderful insight into the world of words and the emotional intelligence that is attached to them. But it has to be said that these people work at the top end of the spectrum. Although there is something for everyone, you do not attend workshops with David or John and expect to pick up a few 'good tips on management'. These are significant life-changing break-throughs which give hope for us all that there are people out there professionally pushing the barriers of the envelope.

The final point to mention here is probably the old chestnut of the differences between coaching and mentoring. Having discussed this at length over the past decade with many of my colleagues I think the consensus is that there are more similarities between coaching and mentoring that there are differences. The key difference, as far as I can see, is that I have yet to come across an organisation that uses mentoring where the line manager is the mentor. However, I have come across many organisations where the line manager is the coach. This is dealt with when we look at the definition of coaching below.

Coaching qualifications

Coaching in the UK has gone through a huge transformation in the past ten years or so. In a business sense it has transformed from a business skills application to a performance management and leadership style approach, using the skills more closely aligned to counselling. The other aspect that has come on in leaps and bounds is the area of executive coaching which in many respects has taken the place of mentoring senior managers and directors. Many organisations still use mentoring in graduate recruitment programmes and the education sector makes extensive use of mentors. The issue of standards is still unresolved in the area of coaching in the context mentioned above, although the European Mentoring and Coaching Council has developed their own Code of Ethics (see Appendix 1). Prior to this comes a plethora of qualifications which split predominately into two areas: certified programmes and accredited programmes. Certified programmes, in the academic sense, mean that the programme is acknowledged and recognised by a university but is not actually a university qualification, whereas accreditation is acknowledged, issued and on many occasions actually delivered by the university. The University of Strathclyde was the first formal university in Britain to certify a coaching approach through its Certificate of Professional Development from the Department of Lifelong Learning. There has since been a number of other universities that have followed suit and more recently the Institute of Leadership and Management, a division of City & Guilds, has also developed an approach which is aimed more at accrediting centres to run qualifications rather than actually qualifying individuals as coaches.

The rise in the demand for coaching qualifications over the past ten years or so has coincided with three major factors, the first being the influence of the United States and the trends from the International Coaching Federation and Coach-U, both founded in the United States and whose early coaching style is rather more directive than that of their UK counterparts. The second factor is the number of UK organisations that have gone through downsizing since the early 1990s (the post-Thatcher boom), because of which individuals have had to increase their skills in other areas, executive coaching being one of them. The third factor lies in the workplace, and in particular the demand for getting more out of less people, leading to the drive for improved performance. Managers and team leaders now have to do what they should have been doing in the first place, that is enable others to carry out these activities. All of this has led to a rise in the demand for qualifications in the coaching market. At the time of the publication of this book, the following academic establishments provide coaching qualifications:

- Derby University – The National Coaching Register
- Middlesex University – Academy of Executive Coaching
- The Open College Network – The Coaching Academy
- The Open College Network – The UK College of Life Coaching
- Oxford Brookes – Chartered Institute of Personnel and Development
- University of Portsmouth – Performance Consultants
- Sheffield Hallam – Sheffield Hallam School of Business and Finance
- University of Strathclyde – The School of Coaching
- University of Strathclyde – IC International
- University of Strathclyde – CFM Consulting Ltd

- Warwick University – The Football Association
- Institute of Leadership & Management (ILM) – ILM Centres
- OCR – Coaching Futures

Further details of the above courses can be obtained from CFM Consulting Ltd (*www.coachingformore.co.uk*) or the Coaching and Mentoring Network (*www.coachingnetwork .org.uk*).

Definition of coaching

Coaching is a management skill and is distinct from mentoring, training and counselling. Each has a role in the workplace and it is useful to establish how they may be appropriately applied. Outlined below are some working definitions.

Coaching

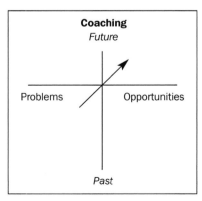

Coaching is the art of facilitating the development, learning and enhanced performance of another.

This operates on a very large scale ranging from a non-directive (pull) to a directive (push) approach. It is always proactive and as a coach you do not always need any knowledge of the subject being coached. You do, however, need a degree of competence in the field of coaching. It mainly falls into three areas:

- *Traditional.* The traditional approach is used to help executives learn how to define tasks and processes. This form of coaching looks more like training. It can be used, for example, to teach managers presentation skills, conflict resolution ability or assertiveness. The coach must know the subject inside out. They are there to build the knowledge and skills of candidates through demonstration, practice and feedback. Evaluating the success of the traditional method can be done by assessing improvements in skills.

- *Transitional.* Transitional coaching looks very different to the traditional approach and is used for different reasons. In traditional coaching, the coach should know all the answers, but with a transitional style, this is not possible or desirable. This method should be applied if there has been a large-scale change in your organisational structure or approach that means the team or department needs to find successful new ways of working. The coach's role is to pose questions, but not to provide answers. The process is designed to help the organisation work out the best solution to a specific situation.

- *Transformational.* Transformational coaching is aimed at very senior levels, and in some respects is the most challenging of all the three approaches. The aim is to enable individuals and/or entire organisations to envisage and move towards completely new ways of working. Often the transformational option is appropriate when a company or an individual has a clear vision of the future and wants to build a bridge from that vision to where they currently are. It often calls for 'blue sky' thinking – an uncluttered approach.

Mentoring

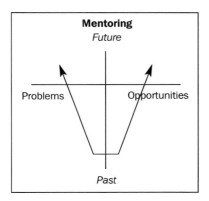

As can be seen from the graph the skill of the mentor comes from past experiences and is broad-based unlike training which has a more targeted background. Mentors can also provide information regarding the cultural and political attributes of people and situations. The mentor's skills can be used to capitalise on future opportunities or overcome past problems.

This is fundamentally different to coaching in so far as the mentor usually is someone more senior, has experience in the field and has a degree of success in the context of work. It is still proactive and it utilises some of the techniques of coaching.

Counselling

This is executed by a qualified (to varying degrees) practitioner and is reactive in that its application is after the event that caused concern. The skills that are required, while similar to both of the above, are used in a different domain.

At the medical end of the counselling spectrum is the psychiatrist. This person is medically trained and qualified and has to have three years' pragmatic experience. They normally have a psychological work practice, and will very often refer the work on to other practitioners. They therefore usually just analyse.

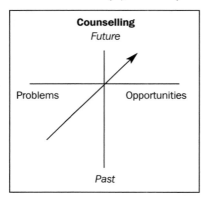

The second area is that of the psychologist. This person may or may not be medically qualified. They primarily concern themselves with studying human behaviour but they have not necessarily done human work.

The third area is that of the psychoanalyst requiring up to seven years' training. Psychoanalysts specialise in self-analysis and very often use non-directive techniques. They therefore strike up their own policy about how they should approach things and, as you might suspect, are not medically trained.

The fourth area is the psychotherapist. A psychotherapist has no medical training but does have five to six years' practical experience as a rule, and generally heals the psyche as opposed to any particular part of the body. They generally deal with history and the past, and usually work in conjunction with doctors or medical practitioners.

From a coaching perspective we very often deal with what is happening in the present and the future and may use questioning techniques to allow people to raise awareness of their past. However, it is not the coach's role to enter the domain of the past with a view to either contain, challenge or condone any behaviours or activities that they may find.

Training

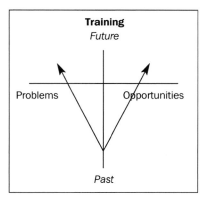

As can be seen from the graph, training usually is driven by a past need in today's corporate world. Usually, it has a directive approach and drives the student down a particular prescribed route. This may be to prepare them for:

- the future, e.g. induction; or
- to rectify a past problem of poor performance, i.e. remedial training of a process.

Most 'soft skills' are reactive – leadership training being a case in point. It can be administered to groups or individuals and is always aimed at improving situations and people for the future. It should also be pointed out that training should not be seen as an end but as a means to an end, and as such other approaches should follow and support it.

Planning a coaching intervention or programme

At some stage in your coaching career it is inevitable that you will need to have to conduct either a coaching intervention or develop a coaching programme and as such it is worth spending some time planning things out. This section deals with this from two perspectives: first and foremost that of planning a coaching intervention on a one-to-one basis; and secondly that of planning a coaching programme involving some kind of cultural change throughout an organisation.

Planning a coaching intervention

One of the key differences is that the coaching intervention is usually requested, in other words you are contacted to carry out that particular piece of work. This should be through an HR department if you are an external consultant, or you may be an internal consultant and have been contacted by the potential client's sponsoring department. As such you may think there is not a great deal of preparation you can do for this. However, nothing could be further from the truth. As a coach you need to be quite clear in your mind what your coaching style is and what your approach is – the whole of Chapter 3 is devoted to the preparation of the coach to ensure that you are in the right frame of mind prior to the coaching session. However, for the present we need to concentrate on ensuring that we are comfortable with our coaching style, our approach and those aspects of contracting that we need to give due diligence to before we even start coaching.

Give some thought to how you are going to prepare yourself for the coaching intervention itself:

- How are you going to take notes?
- How are you going to come across?
- What is your proportion of talking to listening?
- How are you going to offer guidance or advice?
- What reference material are you going to refer to?

All of these need to be clear in your mind before you even start to think about your coaching engagement.

Another aspect of your preparation is to get yourself familiar with the particular organisation that you will be working for.

- What is their code of practice, i.e. the standards to which they work?
- What is their ethos – their mission, aims, objectives?
- How do they work?
- What is their corporate culture?
- How are things done around here?
- What is their dress code?
- How could you arrive within this organisation and typify a professional approach?

These are some of the questions that you need to be concerning yourself with prior to a coaching intervention, whether you are an external consultant contracted to the organisation or an internal consultant brought in by the client's sponsoring department.

This then leads us on to how you will actually contract. During the contracting stage – discussed further in Chapter 3 – you need to consider certain aspects such as your approach.

- While you might have a non-directive style, where does this fit with what the client is actually looking for?

- Are you in fact the right coach?

- Are they looking for a coach with experience in a particular subject area and therefore can offer guidance and advice? Do you have this? If not, who could you refer the client on to thus maintaining your professional approach?

- How will you discuss the terms of confidentiality with the client? What will go outside of the room and who will have access to it?

It is important to stress that this is a balanced approach and as such you are encouraged to go with the flow during the coaching intervention and not make pre-judgements that could jeopardise or bias the conversation and outcomes. This is the area where there is very little preparation to do other than that outlined in Chapter 3 in the section on the preparation of the coach which deals with your mental state prior to coaching.

Finally, you need to consider some ideas for follow-up. How are you going to ensure that your client does actually do what they are supposed to do? Your approach and style may be such that it is not your role or your job even to enforce action plans or ensure that they are carried out. My own approach is to use electronic media and phone calls to keep in touch with the client to let them know that they are supported through this process, although the responsibility for execution of the process finally rests with them.

Planning a coaching programme

This is usually undertaken on a mass scale by comparison to intervention planning and generally proceeds along the following lines. Say an organisation makes a decision to develop a coaching culture within various departments and contacts the HR department to assist in the planning, development and roll-out. At this stage it is key to find out from the organisation what it actually is they want to do.

- What is it they are actually calling for?
- Do they just want to coach a few people?
- Do they want to develop coaching as a management style?
- Do they actually want to use coaching in the performance management process?

If any of the above are applicable then the coaching approach must be aligned with the particular requirements of the client. Along with giving consideration to what the overall objective is, you have to consider who the primary audiences are for each respective programme that is going to be run. There is, it is fair to say, a degree of snobbery in the corporate world that means that senior managers like to be treated differently to middle managers and the middle managers like to be treated differently to first line managers, and as such you might take a slightly different approach (or a very different approach) to accommodate the requirements of each of the respective audiences. Consultation with both the sponsoring department and the respective audiences will help overcome any difficulties here.

During this consultation process it is important to keep an eye open for what support is needed and to a certain extent we can learn from the training/planning examples that have been used in the past where we generally tended towards attitude, knowledge and skills. All training should be designed to achieve changes in attitude, knowledge or skills, or any mix of the three. Getting it wrong can be costly. Imagine if someone has a 'couldn't care less' attitude to the subject they were being trained in. Sending them on a training course would not be an appropriate development route, in the same way that someone who knows the highway code (that is, has the theoretical knowledge) would not have the practical skill to drive a car.

So let's go back to the aspect of coaching – what is the attitude of the participants in the first place? Do they see coaching as just another task they have to do along with their 'day job' or do they actually see it as a tool to help them do that 'day job'? Obviously the latter is the preferred approach, but not everybody comes to a workshop with this starting point. For that reason there may need to be roadshows and briefings by the senior management team to develop the right attitude to ensure that coaching is embedded within the culture of the organisation.

At this stage I would suggest we try not to run before we can walk. Do not be 'too off the wall', that is too innovative in your approach, if there is an attitudinal restriction that is causing problems. You need to develop people along the route generally, so they can make up their own minds that coaching is the approach they wish to take. It is also worth keeping an eye on what cultural aspects are in existence and will need to change. For example, very often in a finance department under the audit services you find that the cultural aspect of compliance is rife, as one would expect. A compliance culture is not necessarily conducive to coaching and unless coaching is positioned alongside as a way of supporting compliance and obtaining buy-in then you will have difficulty actually getting this particular cultural change within that department. Only then can we start to look at the programme design.

Having already covered attitude, we will now look at the knowledge that needs to be imparted in any programme. The skills side of things will be addressed later, but at this stage what are the key areas of knowledge that people need to obtain? Very often you find organisations will align themselves successfully with one preferred coaching style. Sir John Whitmore's approach in the GROW model has been used in many organisations as a very simple, but not simplistic, tool and people generally tend to build their coaching approach around this. (It has to be said that this is an exceptional cornerstone with which to start. The tool itself is discussed in Chapter 4 on maintaining the coaching along with the many other tools that can be used to add to the GROW model at later stages of cultural development.)

However, you have to keep in mind that while you might be able to fill somebody with all the knowledge in the world, it does not necessarily mean that they can deploy the skills that are required. For example, as noted above, you can read the highway code until you know it back to front and inside out but it does not necessarily mean that you can actually drive a car competently. Somewhere down the line skills need to be practised, and most coaching organisations will actually allow for a gap between certain parts of the programme to allow managers and participants to coach each other so they can experience what they are being taught. Also, more and more participants are being exposed to being coached themselves so they can see what it is like from the receiving end. Both of these methods are particularly astute in the way that they actually hone the skills and develop the knowledge. Bear in mind that there needs to be a certain degree of follow-up – in many cases where coaching is used to reinforce training after a course retention values are significantly higher.

The next aspect to consider is evaluation, keeping in mind that we are still at the planning stage. How are you going to evaluate the coaching to ensure that you have actually hit the mark as requested by the sponsor, and how are you going to ensure that you add value for money or provide a return on investment? Chapter 6 on evaluating the coaching goes into this in much greater detail, but it is worth considering at this stage what it is that you need to do.

The final point to consider if you are developing a cultural change within an organisation is that nothing will thrive on neglect – there needs to be a certain degree of maintenance.

Continually upgrading or maintaining the coaching and developing models of continuing professional development and supervision will help this happen. This is touched on in Chapter 7. As a parting shot it is worth reminding people that whether you are planning a coaching intervention or planning a coaching programme it is not necessary to reinvent the wheel. There are many examples of best practice around and most of what is developed in the field of coaching is developed via networks. Make good use of these networks and cut down on your workload as far as planning is concerned.

Note

1.   However, a more recent study of coaching in the UK is available from the Chartered Institute of Personnel and Development (tel: 020 8971 9000; website: *http:// www.cipd.co.uk*).

Further reading

Argyris, C. and Schön, D. (1992) *Theory in Practice*. Jossey-Bass Wiley.

Flaherty, James (1999) *Coaching – Evoking Excellence in Others*. Butterworth-Heinemann.

Hargrove, Robert (1995) *Masterful Coaching*. Pfeiffer Wiley.

Heron, John (1990) *Helping the Client – A Creative Practical Guide*. Sage.

Heron, John (1999) *The Complete Facilitator's Handbook*, 2nd edn. Kogan Page.

2

Basic skills

Listening

Active listening

Reflective listening has its roots in the fields of counselling and psychotherapy, particularly in Carl Rogers' 'client centered' therapy (1995a). This is not to say people in organisations should become therapists, but rather that this one therapeutic skill can be very useful in many everyday work situations.

Reflective listening is used in situations where you are trying to help the speaker deal with something. As you will see, it is very similar to what Tannen (1994) would call 'rapport-talk'.

There are two major aspects of client-centred listening – the 'listening orientation' and the 'reflective technique'.

Listening orientation

In listening orientation, the listener adopts what Rogers (1995a) called 'the Therapist's hypothesis'. This is the belief that the capacity for self-insight, problem-solving and growth resides primarily in the speaker. This means that the central questions for the listener are not 'What can I do for this person?' or even 'How do I see this person?' but rather 'How does this person see themselves and their situation?'

Rogers and others have made the underlying orientation of the listener more specific by noting that it contains four components: empathy, acceptance, congruence and concreteness.

Empathy is the listener's desire and effort to understand the recipient of help from the recipient's internal frame of reference rather than from some external point of view, such as theory, a set of standards or the listener's preferences. The empathetic listener tries to get inside the other's thoughts and feelings. The idea is to obtain a specific rather than a general understanding of the situation from the other person's point of view.

Expressed verbally and non-verbally through messages such as 'I follow you', 'I'm with you' or 'I understand', empathy is the listener's effort to hear the person more deeply, accurately and non-judgementally. A person who sees that a listener is really trying to understand his or her meanings will be willing to explore his or her problems and self more deeply.

Empathy is surprisingly difficult to achieve. We all have a strong tendency to advise, tell, agree or disagree from our own point of view.

Acceptance is closely related to empathy. Acceptance means having respect for a person for simply being a person. Acceptance should be as *unconditional* as possible. This means that the listener should avoid expressing agreement or disagreement with what the other person says. This attitude encourages the other person to be less defensive and to explore aspects of self and the situation they might otherwise keep hidden.

Congruence refers to openness, frankness and genuineness on the part of the listener. The congruent listener is in touch with themselves. If angry or irritated, for example, the congruent person admits to having this feeling rather than pretending not to have it (perhaps because they are trying to be accepting). They communicate what they feel and know, rather than hide behind a mask. Candour on the part of the listener tends to evoke candour in the speaker. When a person comes out from behind a façade, the other is more likely to as well.

In some cases, the principle of congruence can be at odds with the principles of empathy and acceptance. For example, if the listener is annoyed with the other person, they probably have to suspend empathy and acceptance until they sort things out.

Concreteness refers to focusing on specifics rather than vague generalities. Often, a person who has a problem will avoid painful feelings by being abstract or impersonal, using expressions like 'sometimes there are situations that are difficult' (which is vague and abstract), or 'most people want …' (which substitutes others for oneself). The listener can encourage concreteness by asking the speaker to be more specific. For example, instead of agreeing with a statement like 'You just can't trust a manager. They care about themselves first and you second', you can ask what specific incident the speaker is referring to.

In active listening, it is important not only that the listener has an orientation involving the four qualities of empathy, acceptance, congruence and concreteness, but that the speaker feels that the listener has that orientation. Consequently, a good listener tries to understand how the other is experiencing the interaction and attempts to shape their responses so that the other person understands where they are coming from. Furthermore, the listener must be prepared to deviate from the four principles if that's what the other person wants. For example, if the other person asks for an opinion, the listener should give it, rather than avoid it as implied by the principles of empathy and acceptance.

The technique of reflection

A listener can implement the elements of listening orientation through a method known as reflection. In reflection, the listener tries to clarify and restate what the other person is saying. This can have a threefold advantage: (1) it can increase the listener's understanding of the other person; (2) it can help the other to clarify their thoughts; and (3) it can reassure the other that someone is willing to attend to his or her point of view and wants to help.

Listening orientation and reflection are mutually reinforcing. Empathy, acceptance, congruence and concreteness contribute to the making of reflective responses. At the same time, reflective responses contribute to the development and perception of the listening orientation.

Some principles of reflective listening are as follows:

- more listening than talking;

- responding to what is personal rather than to what is impersonal, distant or abstract;

- restating and clarifying what the other has said, and not asking questions or telling what the listener feels, believes or wants;

- trying to understand the feelings contained in what the other is saying, not just the facts or ideas;

- working to develop the best possible sense of the other's frame of reference while avoiding the temptation to respond from the listener's frame of reference;

- responding with acceptance and empathy, not with indifference, cold objectivity or fake concern.

Responding to what is personal means responding to things the other person says about him- or herself rather than about other people, events or situations. If a co-worker said, 'I'm worried that I'll lose my job', the reflective listener would try to focus on the worried 'I' rather than on the job situation. A response such as 'It's scary' would be better than 'Maybe the cutbacks won't affect you.' When the listener responds to personal statements rather than impersonal ones, the other usually stays at the personal level, exploring further aspects of his or her experience, improving his or her understanding of the situation and developing a more realistic, active approach to solving problems.

Because the goal of the process is for the other person, rather than the listener, to take responsibility for the problem, reflective listening means responding to, rather than leading, the other. Responding means reacting from the other's frame of reference to what the other has said. In contrast, leading means directing the other person to talk about things the helper wants to see the other explore. The responsive listener addresses those things the other person is currently discussing, often testing his or her understanding of the other by restating or clarifying what the other has just said. This usually encourages the other to build on the thoughts and feelings he or she has just expressed and to explore further.

While questions can be responsive rather then leading, they very often work to limit the other's initiative by focusing attention on something the listener feels should be discussed. Though small, the question 'Why?' can be particularly damaging, since it defies the other to find a justification or logical explanation that is acceptable to the helper. Instead, you might try: 'That's interesting – can you tell me more about it?'

Perhaps more important, the reflective listener tries to respond to feelings, not just to content. Feelings emerge in the emotional tone that the speaker expresses, such as anger, disappointment, fear, joy, elation or surprise. Content refers to ideas, reasons, theories, assumptions and descriptions – to the *substance* of the speaker's message. As Tannen (1994) notes, in 'troubles-talk' the speaker is often not looking for the solution of the surface problem but rather for a way to deal with the emotional and social ramifications.

In addition, Carl Rogers (1995b) notes that a person who receives response at the emotional level has 'the satisfaction of being deeply understood' and can go on to express more feelings, eventually getting 'directly to the emotional roots' of their problem.

Usually, the listener can be most in touch with the other's frame of reference by responding to feelings that are expressed rather than unexpressed. Since many people do not state their emotions explicitly, this may mean responding to the emotional tone that they express implicitly.

It is extremely important for the reflective listener to respond to negative and ambivalent feelings because this communicates that the listener accepts the unpleasant side of the other's experience and is willing to join in exploring it. Such acceptance provides a major release for a person who has previously felt it necessary to suppress negative feelings. The energy that has been used to keep these feelings in check can now be devoted to exploring the problem.

The next step is to actually try it out on people. It will be awkward at first. It is really hard to say reflective things in a way that sounds natural for you. But you'll find that even bad attempts tend to produce immediate results, maybe because most people rarely have the experience of being listened to in this way.

Advantages of reflective listening

Used appropriately, reflective listening may provide three very positive results:

■ *The listener gains information.* Reflective listening encourages the speaker to talk about more things in greater depth than he or she would be likely to do in simply responding to directive questions or suggestions. Such depth of discussion often exposes underlying problems, including ones the speaker had not recognised previously.

■ *The relationship between the two people develops.* The elements of listening orientation – empathy, acceptance, congruence and concreteness – are likely to increase as the reflective listening process continues. These are the ingredients for an open, trusting relationship.

■ *The activity arouses and channels motivational energy.* Because the listener is an accepting and encouraging partner but leaves the initiative for exploring and diagnosing the problem mainly up to the speaker, a normal outcome of the process is that the speaker will recognise new avenues for action and will begin making plans to pursue them.

Some dangers to avoid

■ *Stereotyped reactions* – constantly repeating a phrase like 'you feel that ...' or 'you're saying that ...'

■ *Pretending understanding* – if you 'get lost' in the conversation say 'Sorry, I didn't get that. What are you saying?' Be honest.

■ *Overreaching* – ascribing meanings that go far beyond what the other has expressed, such as by giving psychological explanations or by stating interpretations that the other considers to be exaggerated or otherwise inaccurate.

- *Under-reaching* – repeatedly missing the feelings that the other conveys or making responses that understate them.

- *Long-windedness* – giving very long or complex responses. These emphasise the listener's massive effort to understand more than they clarify the other person's point of view. Short, simple responses are more effective.

- *Inattention to non-verbal clues* – facing or leaning away from the other, not maintaining eye contact, looking tense or presenting a 'closed' posture by crossing the arms are only a few of the non-verbal cues a listener should avoid. 'Correct' verbal responses are of little use when accompanied by non-verbal signals that contradict them.

- *Violating the other person's expectations* – giving reflective responses when they are clearly not appropriate to the situation. For example, if the other person asks a direct question and obviously expects an answer, simply answering the question is often best. In other words, if someone says: 'What time is it?' you don't usually say 'You're feeling concerned about the time?'

'Blessed is the man who having nothing to say abstains from giving us worthy evidence of that fact.'

George Eliot

The choices made by the reflective listener

The reflective listener's choices are summarised in Figure 2.1.

Questioning

The four cornerstones of questioning

Questioning is central to assisting people in their learning. This is distinct from a teaching mode, where questioning is used as a test to discover whether people have learnt what they were supposed to learn. In the coaching context, much that the coach will do revolves around questioning of one sort or another. If questioning is of such importance, it is useful to have in mind some things that might be questioned. Essentially, these emerge from whatever it is the client is speaking of, but here we shall consider some general directions in which questioning can go.

The starting point is that the clients will be relating ideas they have about a situation, feelings they have about it, or actions they have taken or propose to take. These will come up whenever clients are either speaking of something they want to develop or reporting on their progress with some previously established learning goal. Whether it is ideas, feelings or actions of which they are speaking, clients may be asked questions in one or more of four directions. These directions can be described as: back towards the histories, ahead towards the consequences, above in relation to the

The listener's choice of focus	Choice of what to respond to	Choice of how to respond	Choice of level to respond to	Type of feelings to respond to
The listener's own point of view	Events and conditions in the other person's life	Lead the other by giving opinions, advice or interpretations	Content	Positive feelings
	People in the other person's life	Lead the other by asking questions		

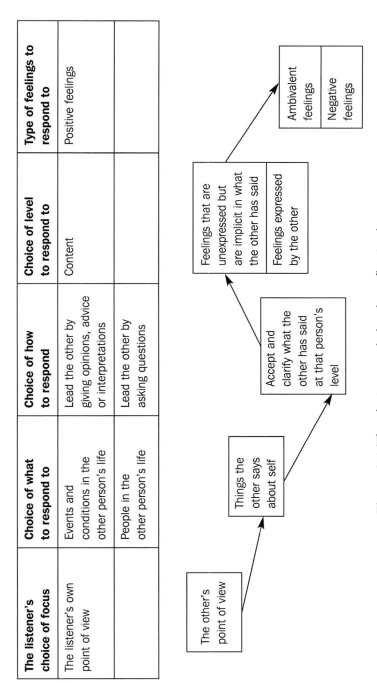

The other's point of view

Things the other says about self

Accept and clarify what the other has said at that person's level

Feelings that are unexpressed but are implicit in what the other has said

Feelings expressed by the other

Ambivalent feelings

Negative feelings

Figure 2.1 The choices made by the reflective listener.

bigger picture or below in relation to the assumptions on which they are based. Figure 2.2 shows how these four directions are linked.

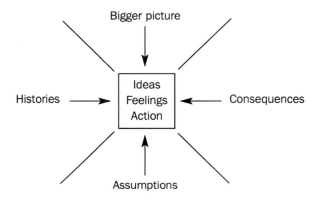

Figure 2.2 Four directions in questioning.

Histories

Any idea, feeling or action will have some history. Something will have led to it. Asking about this (indeed 'What led up to this?' is only one, generic, question for exploring this direction) opens up potential avenues of learning. The point here is that the particular idea, feeling or action may not be beneficial to clients in their situation. If this is so, recognising how they came to have it reveals it as less of a 'given' and can therefore make it easier to change.

Consequences

In the opposite direction, there will be consequences of one sort or another to any idea, feeling or action. At the point at which questions are being asked, the consequences will not yet have been revealed. What is being asked about, therefore, are the learner's thoughts about what those consequences will be. Answering such questions may reveal to them aspects they have not previously thought about.

That is the case with actions; however, though it may be a less familiar concept, the *ideas* the learner holds and the *feelings* they have will also have consequences. For instance, feeling nervous or embarrassed about some action they plan to take may well have consequences for how effective they are able to be. Similarly, the idea that they need someone else's authority to talk to people in another function has direct consequences for how they are going to proceed. Recognising this, they may decide to drop that idea as unnecessarily restrictive.

Bigger picture

Whatever ideas, feelings or actions are the focus of a client's attention will have a place in a bigger picture. In some cases, this will be obvious and explicit, as when they are discussing steps in their development of a particular ability. However, even here, that ability will itself have a place in a larger scheme. For instance, it will be part of the client's progression in the organisation or in their profession.

It is often useful to revisit such connections, which, after all, are seen by different people in different ways. Viewing issues from other people's perspective can help complete the bigger picture and often can provide the breakthrough that clients are looking for.

Assumptions

Whatever is being spoken about will be underwritten by a set of assumptions. More often than not, these will be unexamined and often totally outside the client's awareness. Many people have recognised that one of the most fruitful activities for individual and organisational creativity is to seek out unnecessary and limiting assumptions. The Post-it note, for example, was a triumph over the assumption that glue was meant to stick things together so that they stayed stuck. The process of 'turning over the stones' to examine what is underneath them can be very revealing. It is also, though, an unfamiliar activity for most people. However, this gives an advantage to those who do it.

The best place to look for assumptions is where a limitation is being experienced. For instance, a client may feel blocked from moving a personal project ahead because help is needed from another function. This is underpinned by the assumption that someone else's authority is needed before people in the other function can be approached. As such assumptions are identified they can be challenged. There is always any number of assumptions that can be open to question.

In fact, it will be found that any assumption stands on a further, deeper level of assumptions. Those, too, can be questioned. This is not to say that all assumptions should be junked. There is nothing wrong with assumptions. Our individual and social worlds are built on them. The issue here is that, if unexamined, they can unnecessarily limit us, as if we were believing something we do not actually, on reflection, really believe in.

In order to describe these different directions of questioning we have taken them one at a time. However, a question posed from any one direction can then lead to questions from other directions. We could ask, for instance, about the history of an underlying assumption or its likely consequences and where it fits into a bigger picture. In other words, this process suggests an endless series of things to question. What guides the choice of any line of questioning, as of any individual question, is the requirement that it benefit the client.

Sample questions

We have given some examples of questions in the four areas below.

Histories

1. Tell me about a coaching session that has gone well.

2. How have you dealt with this situation previously?

3. What have you learnt from your experiences?

4. What did you have in mind when you did that?

5. Give me an example of when that happened in the past.

6. How have you dealt with this in the past?

7. How has this situation arisen before?

Consequences

1. What do you think will happen if you did/did not do that?

2. How does this affect others around you?

3. What did you hope to achieve?

4. How do your actions affect other team members?

5. What impact does that have on ...?

6. How does that make people feel?

Assumptions (to challenge)

1. What do you think would happen if you did this?

2. What did you expect would happen?

3. How did you think this would resolve the situation?

4. What reasons lie behind not delegating/allocating work?

Assumptions (listen for)

1. 'We've never been allowed to do that before'.

2. 'We can't do that'.

3. 'This is how I think they feel'.

4. 'We've always done it that way before'.

The bigger picture

1. What do you think about ...?

2. How do you feel you have achieved it?

3. How do you think you can change the situation?

4. Where are there problems?

5. How does the way you act differ from other managers?

6. How does the way you work fit in with other team members?

7. What is expected of you compared with other team members?

8. Where does this fit in with the departmental objectives?

9. Where does this fit in with 'living the vision'?

10. How would they view this in ... [e.g. the finance department]?

11. What is the customer expectation?

The strategic questioning process

In order to achieve a long-term objective, it is commonplace to have a strategy – the 'what' in what you are going to do. Once the strategy is in place you can then get to grips with the tactical plan – the 'how' in how we are going to achieve it.

In this section we offer some guidance on pulling the strategy together by way of asking the right questions. The strategic questioning process is split into three levels – describing the issue, digging deeper and creating the strategic statement. The idea is to get enough information to pull together a very loose mind-map (see Buzan, 1989). Once the mind-map is created you can create a paragraph that encompasses the 'what' in what you are going to do. In any strategy the end result should be understood by anyone who reads it. It should be clear, generate enthusiasm and generate hope for the future.

The first level: describing the issue or problem

1. *Focus questions* – gather information that is already known. When you look at the issue, what do you see that concerns you?

2. *Observation questions* – what do you see? What do you read about this situation? What information do you need to gather about this situation?

3. *Analysis questions* – thinking questions. What is the relationship of ... to ... ?

4. *Feeling questions* – how has this situation affected you? Your feelings? How has it affected feelings about your family, community, the world?

The second level: strategic questions ... digging deeper

Now we start asking questions that increase the motion. The mind takes off, creating new information, synthesising, moving from what is known to the realm of what could be.

1. *Visioning questions* – are concerned with identifying one's ideals, values and dreams. How would you like to be? What is the meaning of this situation in your life?

2. *Change questions* – address how to get a more ideal situation. How might changes you would like to see come about? Name as many ways as possible. What changes have you seen or read about? Here you are trying to find the person's change view, which will greatly impact their strategies for change.

3. *Considering all the alternatives* – what are all the possible ways you could accomplish these changes? How could you reach that goal? What are the other ways? What would it take for you to do whatever it is you need to do?

4. *Consider the consequences* – how does your first alternative affect the others in the context? What would be the effect on the environment? What political effect would you anticipate from each alternative?

5. *Consider the obstacles* – what would you need to change in order for alternative 'a' to be done? What keeps you from doing ... ? Decisions become clear around this point. Are you getting a sense of what you want to do? What is in the way of clarity?

6. *Personal inventory and support questions* – what support do you need to do ... ? What support would you need to work for this change?

7. *Personal action questions* – who do you need to talk to about your vision? How can you get others to work on this?

The third level: creating the strategic statement

Plot the answers to the questions on a 'mind-map' (see Buzan, 1989). Leave the 'mind-map' for a day or so and then go back to it. Use the answers to create a strategic statement. It should be around a paragraph in length and have absolute clarity from many perspectives.

Asking the right questions can help clients think more clearly, take more responsibility for themselves and accomplish their goals more easily, so argues Marilee Goldberg, the originator of question-based therapy. In her book *The Art of the Question* (1997), Goldberg provides a guide to clinicians for incorporating question-based therapy into their work, including pertinent case study vignettes and illustrated psycho-educational materials for their clients.

Assessing your mentoring style

Summary of basic helping styles

When a mentor is asked for help by a client the response will depend on two factors:

1. The way in which the mentor first views the situation:
   - is their concern for the client (client-centred), or
   - is their concern for the problem (problem-centred)?

2. The way in which the mentor works on the problem:

   - do they work on their own (excludes the client), or
   - with the client (includes the client)?

When these factors are combined it can be seen that there are four basic 'helping' styles that can be adopted and each will have a different effect. They are: *telling*, *advising*, *manipulating* and *counselling* (see Figure 2.3). Each of these styles is described more fully below:

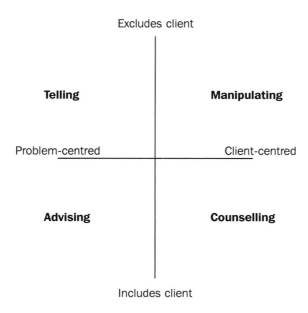

Excludes client

Telling   Manipulating

Problem-centred   Client-centred

Advising   Counselling

Includes client

Figure 2.3 The basic helping styles.

1. *Telling.* The mentor who gives help by 'telling' the client what to do is problem-centred and excludes the client from the problem-solving process. This style is frequently adopted by technical experts whose skill and knowledge enable them to give the 'right answer'.

2. *Advising.* The mentor who helps by 'giving advice' is problem-centred and includes the client in the problem-solving. The adviser frequently develops options and then asks the client to select the one they favour. The danger is that the adviser will offer solutions requiring their own expertise which is not available to the client.

3. *Manipulating.* The mentor who uses a 'manipulating' style is apparently client-centred but in fact excludes

the client from the problem-solving process. The manipulator uses the client to satisfy their own needs and wants to keep the client in a highly dependent role. Manipulative helpers can often be recognised by their tendency to offer help before anyone requests it.

4.   *Counselling*. Counselling is a style of helping which is client-centred and involves the client in solving the problem. It is significantly different from the other three styles and aims to help the client find solutions to their own problems.

Assessing my mentoring style

Outlined below is a self-assessment activity designed to help mentors to assess their mentoring style.

Aims

■ To assess current mentoring style.

■ To identify any changes that need to be made to current mentoring style.

■ To agree a course of action for changing current mentoring style.

Method

1.   Identify three situations where you recently 'helped' another person. (This could be a colleague, friend or member of staff.)

2. Using the grid from Figure 2.3, place each situation in the appropriate quadrant.

3. Discuss your responses with a colleague or partner and answer the following questions:

    − Which style(s) did you use?

    − Do you tend to use the same style with everyone?

    − How effective or helpful was this style?

    − How do you know it was effective or helpful?

    − What changes, if any, would you like to make to your style?

    − How and when will you make these changes?

    − Who will help you to make these changes?

4. Record the changes you want to make under the following headings:

    − WHAT changes?

    − HOW?

    − WHEN?

    − WHO WILL HELP?

5. Review progress at regular intervals with a colleague or mentor if possible. Alternatively you could ask for feedback from the people you 'help' in future.

Understanding practical learning styles

Learning styles

It is widely accepted that not everyone learns and processes information in the same way. Given the same learning opportunity two people will most likely want very different things to enable them to learn effectively. Accordingly it is possible to become a more effective learner and coach if you have a better understanding of want you need from a learning experience, or how the client learns.

Karen Tidswell and Keith Rogers have designed a package entitled 'Practical Learning Styles' to identify what each individual needs as a learner. In particular it assesses:

- the way you prefer information to be presented;
- the way you prefer to make sense of information.

The learning style dimensions

The 'Practical Learning Styles' questionnaire is designed to identify learning preferences according to four dimensions. Each dimension has an associated pair of learning styles that are indicated in Table 2.1.

Learning style information

Outlined below is a summary of the learning style information for each dimension, including:

Table 2.1 Learning style dimensions

Dimension	Learning styles
Orientation	This focuses on your instructional preference and assesses whether you are a *realistic* or a *creative* learner. Typically a realistic learner prefers practical courses and likes to learn in small connected chunks whereas a creative learner prefers imaginative courses and gains understanding in large holistic leaps.
Interaction	This focuses on your approach to study and assesses whether you are a *doer* or a *thinker*. Typically a doer likes activity-based learning whereas a thinker likes time to reflect and plan learning.
Representation	This focuses on your mental representation of material to be learned and assesses whether you are a *verbaliser* or a *visualiser*. Typically a verbaliser presents and learns information using words whereas a visualiser prefers to use images and diagrams.
Processing	This focuses on the learning process you use to remember new information and assesses whether you are a *surface* or a *deep processor*. Typically a surface processor likes to learn by rote whereas a deep processor likes to understand underlying concepts.

- the differences between the extremes for each pair of learning styles;
- what the extremes prefer.

Realistic – Creative

This dimension focuses on your *instructional preference* and assesses whether your preferred learning style is that of a *realistic* or *creative* learner. It assesses what kind of data you prefer to learn with – in other words whether you prefer practical or creative courses. This dimension considers whether or not you prefer to:

- concentrate on one thing at a time in order to develop a depth of understanding;
- work on several things at once in order to develop a breadth of understanding.

Doer – Thinker

This dimension focuses on your *approach to study* and assesses whether your preferred learning style is that of a *doer* or a *thinker*. It assesses whether you:

- like action and variety in your learning experiences;
- prefer time alone for reflection and contemplation;
- like learning with others or alone.

Verbaliser – Visualiser

This dimension focuses on your *mental representation* of the material to be learned and assesses whether your preferred learning style is that of a *verbaliser* or a *visualiser*. This dimension determines whether you prefer material to be presented to you in pictures, images and diagrams or whether you prefer the written word to be used. Everyone can use both modes of representation but most people have a defined preference for one over the other.

Surface processor – deep processor

This dimension focuses on the *learning process* that you use to remember new information and assesses whether your preferred learning style us that of a *surface* or a *deep processor*. It determines whether you prefer to learn by memorising facts or by understanding underlying concepts. It examines whether you learn best by using rote learning techniques or by reinterpreting new information in your own words. It also determines whether you learn just enough to get you by or whether you actually enjoy delving deeper than is necessary into new subjects.

The 'Practical Learning Styles' package

Through completing the 'Practical Learning Styles' package from Tidswell and Rogers it is possible to identify your learning preferences. Also it provides greater understanding of the meaning of these preferences and thus enables you to develop your learning style to become a more balanced and flexible learner. Furthermore by establishing your own learning style preferences and undertaking the associated development activities you will be able to tackle new learning tasks with greater efficiency and effectiveness. With that knowledge, from a coach's perspective, you can couch the language you use in terms that make it easier for your client to understand and learn.

The catalytic toolkit

Coaches are no different from any other group of consummate professionals who have a continual thirst and hunger to develop themselves in new areas. In many cases this means reinventing old areas to develop and adapt them so that they fit the new platforms on which they wish to work.

As has been mentioned many times, modern business coaching very often owes its roots to the reactive therapy of counselling and there are many tools and techniques that can be brought over from this particular field. One of the practitioners in the field of counselling that has done more to develop this area than others, although each practitioner has had their part to play, is John Heron, the author of numerous books such as *The Complete Facilitator's Handbook* (1999) and *Helping the Client* (1990). It is from the latter publication that the following coaching tool has been adapted. John has developed an approach called 'The Six Categories' – confronting, supportive, informative, cathartic, prescriptive and catalytic – and while each has a place, in the field of coaching it is the catalytic tool that serves our purpose more than anything else.

The very name catalytic has always been a source of discussion as the definition of the catalyst is something that changes something else while remaining the same itself. In the field of coaching it also causes some degree of confusion – I have yet to meet one coach that has facilitated change in another without them being changed themselves in some way, shape or form, whether it be through learning, understanding, grasping knowledge or improving their skills. However, what John Heron has developed here is a series of approaches based upon a platform that serves the client and coach to enable the client to solve some of their own problems, see some of their own developments and recognise some of their own opportunities. In order to illustrate the catalytic toolkit, it is best to look at the model outlined in Figure 2.4.

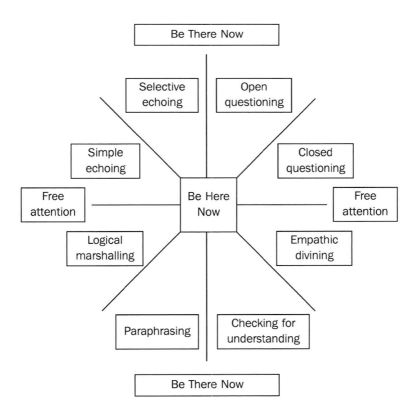

Reprinted by permission of Sage Publications Ltd
(from John Heron, *Helping the Client*, 1990, pp. 130–1).

Figure 2.4 The catalytic toolkit (Heron, 1999).

The first area to look at is right in the centre of the model labelled 'Be Here Now'. While John refers to this as being the everyday mystical position, for many practitioners there is no mystery about it at all. It is all about centring yourself in the present, what many Gestalt therapists refer to as being an empty vessel. It is not about what you actually do, it is about how you are – it's about your demeanour, your approach, your style and, most importantly of all, about your awareness of the present. Certainly, from a physical point of view, it is about being relaxed, being at peace with your environment and your surroundings, but from a mental point of view it is about honing the mind to be sharp and aware of what is currently present so you can intuitively pick up what is going on but not be engulfed by it. Different people have different ways of doing this – the poet David Whyte uses poetry to centre himself prior to an engagement with a client. The chairman of one organisation I am familiar with ensures that he knows exactly where his client has come from prior to actually meeting with him and uses the same discipline himself to 'mentally cleanse' himself prior to going into the meeting with his client.

The second area we need to look at is right on the edge of the model which is about being there now. There are several things that connect here. Firstly, if you have engaged correctly in the previous state, that is being here now, this will invite your client to understand that you are also there for them by the same standard. They will sense and see that everything with you is with them. For the professional coach there is no mystery about this – once again it is about creating peace for themselves so that the individual they are working with can actually sense that peace and take encouragement from it. This is easily recognised when a coach is coaching a client in the area of confidence. First of all the client will actually take confidence from the coach. There then needs to be a migration of the confidence from the coach to the client where the client can become self-sufficient. The client senses that there is no anxiety or animosity, fear or threat in the coach and that it is all about the coach being there now for the client. However, this is one aspect to watch as many clients can often feel that the coach has solved problems, recognised opportunities or made suggestions for them when in actual fact they have not done any such thing. What they have done is carefully and meticulously coached in such a supportive way through being there now that it has enabled the conversation to reach a successful conclusion.

The next area we must look at is the area between the two being here now and being there now, and for me this is the platform that enables the conversation. The coach is not actually listening for any trends at this point, they are not trying to identify opportunities – they are literally giving free attention. There is no hidden agenda on the coach's part but there is the opportunity to pause, summarise, reflect on and question the platform that has been created. Just as a stagehand would dress a stage prior to a theatrical performance this is what is happening between the coach and the client. There is a sense of engagement at a much higher level than most of us are usually aware of, but it is intuitively picked up by the coach and the client. This is where the real coaching occurs.

We next need to look at the eight areas that Heron has outlined in his model, many of which have been around for many years in the field of coaching and counselling. Certainly some of the points are actually highlighted in an old BACIE (British Association for Commercial and Industrial Education) manual that was first produced in 1975 purely for the art of coaching in the workplace.

Let us start with *simple echoing*. The object of the exercise here is actually as stated: you echo back the last words or last few words before pausing for effect. From experience I have never rephrased these words, added any interrogative inflection or implied any judgement as the coach. It has very often proved to be a wake-up call for the client as they then start to look at why you picked that particular area to echo back.

I remember one particular situation where a client was talking about the particular person they wished to improve their working relationship with and they finished with a sentence, which was more of a throw-away line, about the individual's responsibilities. Just by echoing the word responsibilities it set the client off on a completely different line of thought that proved quite fruitful in the end. What had actually happened in this part of the conversation was that when I had reflected the word responsibilities, the client had then added their interpretation to it, having heard it from me, and then investigated that particular aspect as opposed to any steering from me. This is a wonderful example of how simple echoing can facilitate the client to travel down their own journey of learning and find a destination that offers a solution.

Selective echoing is not unlike simple echoing. However, because you have created the platform of giving free attention, your listening is finely tuned to everything that is going on with regard to what the client is saying, what they are doing, how they are being. But as opposed to simple echoing where you echo back something at the end, in this case you are selective and you reflect back something either from the middle or from other aspects of the client's conversation. In essence it is some word or aspect that actually stands out from what you have heard, and once again you wish the client to investigate this, using them as the driving force. There is no interrogation on your part or inflection on your echo – it needs to model this aspect of giving free attention.

Two areas to be aware of here are that selective echoing can be used to follow the speaker into a particular aspect that they are already discussing, but it can also be used to actually change the track of a conversation. It is a particularly useful tool when the client is being very verbose and you wish to move them into another area to raise their awareness about some particular aspect of what they have just said.

The next area to look at is *open questioning* and while this is the aspect most people are familiar with, it is one that doesn't have any correct answers and the fear for most untrained coaches is than an open question will lead to an open answer. The good news for the professional coach is that this is exactly what you want. The opposite of this is *closed questioning*. This is one area that does have a right answer – usually a yes or a no – and the benefit from a coaching point of view of this particular questioning is that it can help confirm or deny a particular aspect before you move on and should be used accordingly. However, there are other aspects of this that we can now start to 'mix up' a bit. For example, we can have closed opening questions – in other words the opening refers to that part of the discussion and we are asking closed questions so we can open up the conversation further. A typical example of this would be, 'Is that something you would like to investigate further?' or 'Are there things in that area that we need to discuss?' Both will give either a yes or no answer and can allow the conversation to open up if you are using it as described earlier.

In the same fashion, you can have open closing questions and the closing once again refers to that particular part of the discussion, so you are now starting to close it down. Typically this would be found in some kind of technique that prompts action from the client, for example: 'So what actions do we need to get down on paper to move this forward?' This is an open question. However, it is used in the closing part of the coaching conversation before moving on to another area.

John Heron makes the point that open questions generally tend to be more catalytic than closed questions because they give more scope for self-directed exploration and discovery, but he also points out that there is no hard and fast rule. The experience of the coach will determine which is the appropriate one to use and it soon will become self-evident, not only which question to ask, but whether you have asked the right question. All questions in this particular area need to be client-centred. Anything other than that will violate the giving free attention platform I mentioned earlier. One can immediately tell when this has been violated because the client becomes defensive, abrasive or just clams up.

The next area takes us into what many sceptics would call the 'tree hugging part' – *empathic divining*, which is literally about divining or digging deeper with a degree of empathy. While I have seen some managers approach this with all the subtlety of a flying mallet, when watching the professional coach in action it is a pure master class. It relates to what is intuitive in the conversation, what is between the lines rather than what is actually said, and it is this particular technique that will determine whether you have created the free attention in such a way that it will allow the individual not to be discouraged by your empathic divining. One comment that I usually pick up on is when people say 'We would never be allowed to get away with that.' That phrase alone says more than the words actually tell us. The phrase is a good litmus test as to how the individual is actually feeling at that particular point in time. When divining with empathy it is important that you express it as a statement and not as a question and this is best done with you almost thinking out loud in a reflective manner, using such expressions as 'From what you are saying, I'm hearing ...' or 'It is interesting how you positioned that.' Sometimes you can actually be so bold as to say 'That's a telling phrase!'

On training courses it is the aspect that people have most fun with because they are aware acutely of their own state of being and of their client's state of being, tone of voice, intonation, etc. However, the key to this technique is not to talk about what is actually said, but to talk about what is between the lines of what is said. In a business sense, if the professional corporate coach can pick this up on an individual basis, it is a short step to actually pick up the cultural environment on a corporate basis.

The next area is *checking for understanding*. Interestingly enough this is the highest point of the scale at the non-directive end of the coaching spectrum – listening to understand. Whereas listening for understanding would imply a passive process, checking for understanding is the more active of the two in this partnership. John Heron suggests that it only be used when the client is groping for words or says something confused or contradictory. However, it can also be used when paraphrasing or summarising. The client will then either agree, disagree or clarify, depending on the situation. It is important to note here that the understanding that you are looking for is the client's understanding, and not your interpretation. Once again, if you are being here now, and therefore being there now and creating that free attention, then the understanding that is derived will be mutual and joint understanding, but it will still be the client's interpretation.

The next area, *paraphrasing*, is where you rephrase in your own words something important that the client has expressed in relation to what they were trying to achieve. This has two benefits. First and foremost, it is an aid to memory. The more you actually paraphrase or repeat back using your own words the more you will gain access to where the memory is stored in the limbic system in your own brain. However, as an added bonus it has shown the client that you are really listening and understanding. It gives a chance to check that their interpretation is still valid and it allows them to alter anything they have said if it has not quite come out the way they intended.

The final area in Heron's model of the catalytic toolkit deals with *logical marshalling*. He defines this as the opposite of empathic divining. Whereas empathic divining dealt with what was 'between the lines', logical marshalling deals with what is 'on the lines' of what the client has actually said. However, I have found it useful to develop this further and to logically marshal the client towards the goal. This allows a degree of direction on the part of the coach, but this is permissible if the contract has been set up accordingly. Very often observers of my own particular style have noted that I am actually quite forceful with the process, but very kind with the client and they see this as being a logical marshalling towards the goal. So from this we can see that we have two aspects: one is logically marshalling by picking up on what the client is actually saying and organising a way forward that fits into the context of the bigger picture, and the second is that it can be used as a tool by the coach to steer people towards their goal.

All in all, what Heron has set out in his model is a particularly useful and beneficial tool for all professional coaches. It is a way of facilitating the conversation and honing the softer skills of coaching in such a way that practitioners can be become professionally competent in this area.

Further reading

Heron, John (1990) *Helping the Client – A Creative Practical Guide*. Sage.

Listening

Knight, Sue (2002) *NLP at Work*. Nicholas Brealey.
Shafir, Rebecca Z. (2000) *The Zen of Listening*. Quest Books.

Assessing your mentoring style

Rogers, Carl (1995a) *Client Centered Therapy*. Trans-Atlantic Publications.
Rogers, Carl (1995b) *On Becoming a Person*. Mariner Books.

Resources

Questioning

For a useful resource book on the topic of questioning see:

Goldberg, Marilee (1997) *The Art of the Question: A Guide to Short-Term Question-Centered Therapy*. Wiley.

Further information

Understanding practical learning styles

For further information on understanding practical learning styles contact Keith Rogers and Karen Tidswell of the Practical Learning Styles Partnership (2002) at:

keith.rogers@rogerstld.plus.com
karentidswell@cedar-ads.com

3

Getting started

The preparation of the coach

In this particular area we are working with what is probably the biggest individual object in the way of becoming a effective professional coach, that is oneself. In many walks of life we prepare for what it is we need to do. For our exams at school or at university we prepare thoroughly, although for some of us that preparation reverts to cramming at the tail end which then leads us to challenge the effectiveness of our revision techniques. In order to pass a driving test we prepare thoroughly through general practice. Now we have to take a theoretical exam before we are allowed to apply for the practical test to demonstrate our competence on the road. Certainly for other major events, holidays, weddings, etc., a fair degree of planning goes in to make sure that the performance is acceptable, and so it should be with coaching.

The performance that we are about to give to our client should be nothing short of professional and as such there needs to be a fair degree of preparation. The first area we need to prepare concerns the tools of our trade, our command of the natural language, the client's mother tongue. In preparation of the second area, the physical environment, we may note that Tony Buzan has commented on numerous occasions that 'nobody has ever had an earth shattering idea when sitting at a desk', yet where do we see most executive coaching performed – at someone's desk. However, if you are not going to use someone's desk area or office to coach them then make sure you have booked the appropriate facilities. In one particular situation I remember working with a client on board the Royal Yacht *Britannia* in Leith and the ambiance and environment just allowed the person to open up completely about many of the things they were currently working on. I have also found, especially in this day of electronic wizardry, that nothing can beat an old-fashioned pen and paper for sketching out ideas and allowing individuals to jot down thoughts and action plans, so it is always a good idea to have these handy. Many of my colleagues actually use a battery of tests, psychometrics, learning styles and competencies, many of which are discussed in this book. However, this just gives due diligence to the client. What we are talking about here is the preparation of you, the coach.

Many years ago Tony Morgan, the former Chief Executive of the Industrial Society, introduced me to David Whyte. David is a man who uses poetry to cross the divide of interpersonal understanding and 'make things real'. After many years of practice I have adopted one of David's approaches in order to prepare for my coaching sessions.

David has for many years been working with a poem by David Wagoner (Chair of Poetry at the University of Washington) based around a native North American teaching story, 'Lost' (quoted in Whyte, 1994: 259), where a young brave or squaw would ask the elder of the tribe, 'What do I do when I'm lost in the forest?'

The response from the elder is illuminating to say the least:

Stand still ...

There is a refreshing quality about the whole story that one can visit with integrity. In other words 'being yourself' – *'wherever you are is called here'*. We are all here, at any point in our lives, and we should acknowledge this as a staging post, where we can be aware of our surroundings and respect our immediate environment. We are also always 'ourselves'. In the coaching sense this is the calming of ourselves, knowing who we are and where we are prior to coaching.

'You must treat it as a powerful stranger' – David talks about this in the following terms: 'The world can nourish you, but it could kill you as soon as look at you.' I believe that we could not only apply this to the world, but any given coaching situation. We must treat any situation with respect and move into it in an appropriate manner. In my model, this is about being alive in the moment and noticing what is going on around us, which in turn removes any interference that might crop up at an inopportune moment during the coaching session.

For some reason children have this ability to be aware of the natural world and pick up on this. My own children, Catriona (10) and Murray (6), were playing at the edge of the woods in a field next to the main A9 north trunk road and were getting far too close to the road for my liking. I called on Catriona to call Murray back from the edge of the field. She instantly recognised the concern in my voice and dutifully called him back, which he obeyed. At no time were either voices raised, but they instinctively knew something was not quite right. This is being in touch with the situation.

Robert Burns typified this in his poem *Tam o' Shanter* in the lines:

> The wind blew as it had blown its last;
> The rattling showers rose on the blast;
> The speedy gleams the darkness swallowed;
> Loud, deep, and long, the thunder bellowed:
> That night, a child might understand,
> The devil had business on his hand.

Here we see that the poet alludes to a child not only seeing but also understanding what we adults miss completely. Children take time to prepare themselves for things that are important for them and somewhere in growing up we adults lose this.

One wonders, then, what interference we can remove to be at one with the environment. Some questions I found useful in this quest were the following:

- What do I see around me?

- What do I observe around me?

- What do I feel around me?

- What do I sense around me?

- What can I hear around me?

I have found that by asking these questions, of which there is more than one answer for each, our state of awareness is raised to the point of extreme focus.

Let us return to Wagoner's poem:

> Stand still,
> The trees ahead and bushes beside you are not lost.
> Wherever you are is called here and you must treat it as a powerful stranger
> You must ask permission to know it and be known. The forest breathes. Listen. It answers, I have made this place around you if you leave it you may come back again saying here.

It is almost saying to us 'Respect me and I will serve you well'. In my model, if we acknowledge and respect our immediate environment, it will help us focus. 'Be at one with me and I will support you' is what I hear from the poem.

> No two trees are the same to Raven, no two branches the same to Wren and if what a tree or a branch does is lost on you, you are surely lost.

This tells us that every part of the environment is different and as such we should be alert to all our surroundings.

> Stand still the forest knows where you are. Stand still, you must let it find you.

This final part of the poem, as David points out, is not an invitation to passivity. It requires skill, maturity and time to cultivate our surroundings so we can be at one with them.

In this sense it means being active, and for a session with my client I would prepare myself in the same way in order to be fully present with focus, openness and energy.

The message in this chapter is about using the right tools to prepare us for coaching both mentally and physically. For me it is a combination of both.

The coaching contract

Coaching contracts

As in most relationships, participants in coaching relationships tend to make implicit, critical assumptions about the relationship: about its purpose, about roles and responsibilities, about coaching methods and about the other party's willingness. When the parties' assumptions aren't aligned, trouble can ensue in the partnership.

'Contracting' for a formal coaching partnership is a way to make these assumptions explicit. By contracting, we mean reaching an explicit operating agreement that provides structure, guidance and alignment for both parties for the duration of the partnership – in essence the 'ground rules'.

This section examines the content of the contracts that individuals should have with their coach, how to make the most of the time available and how to ensure that topics are covered at the right time.

Three important functions of contracting

- *Ensures alignment.* Contracting establishes focus, agreement on desired results, understanding of and adjustment to individual needs and preferences, clarity of roles and responsibilities, and a common language for performance and development.

- *Establishes procedures.* Contracting addresses the steps for realising goals, the coaching methods employed, time frames, boundaries and ground rules, and measurement of progress.

- *Models partnership.* Contracting serves as an effective orientation into the coaching partnership, modelling presence, disclosure, enquiry and commitment to one another's success.

Creating a verbal or written coaching contract is useful for any coaching partnership. It is clearly an important step in coaching interventions of limited duration, such as targeted executive coaching. Contracting is also valuable in the more common ongoing coaching that results from a reporting relationship.

It is even more important to consider the coaching contract when your normal modus operandi is that of a manager.

Two aspects of a contract

Essentially there are two elements in a contract. One element considers the coach as a practitioner and the other element concerns itself with the actual process of coaching.

Coach as practitioner

When working with the coach as a practitioner you may wish to consider drawing up a profile such as in Table 3.1.

The process of coaching

The actual process of coaching may be covered as outlined in Table 3.2.

Table 3.1 Profile of coach as practitioner

Area	Description
Style	Usually non-directive asking questions.
Parameters	Predominately in the field of coaching, but will flag up if the conversation is getting out of my depth.
Tools	Some tools that I may use, e.g. GROW, range of coaching approaches, modelling and note-taking.
Confidentiality	While the conversation is bound by client confidentiality, I reserve the right to challenge unethical/immoral activities or actions.
Session time	Usually in short bursts of 20–25 minutes.
Follow-up	At least once within one week.
Feedback	The client will give feedback to me as the coach after each session.

Table 3.2 The process of coaching

Issue	Question(s) to be answered	Examples
Reason for the coaching	What is the current state of performance and/or development, and the required or desired need to change?	■ To improve unsatisfactory performance in the short term. ■ To prepare for a promotion within 18 months. ■ To promote success on a difficult project.
Specific goal(s) of the coaching	What specifically will the partnership try to accomplish?	■ Bringing monthly sales up to target. ■ Knowledge of planning/budgeting. ■ Improved influence skills.
Coaching method(s) to be used	What will be the predominant method used to achieve the goals of the partnership?	■ Modelling or demonstrations by coach. ■ Regular feedback on performance. ■ Support for developmental activities. ■ Debrief of challenging assignments.
Timing	When will coaching occur?	■ At regular (daily/weekly/monthly) intervals. ■ As needed. ■ Any time, except when either party is working under a deadline.
Measurement of progress	How will the parties assess progress?	■ Eyeball it. ■ Obtain customer feedback. ■ Track regular measures, such as sales revenue.
Duration/conditions of termination	At what point will the coaching relationship end?	■ When the partnership goal is achieved. ■ As long as the person being coached reports to the coach.

The inner game

When *The Inner Game of Tennis* was published in 1975 its author, Tim Gallwey, contributed to coaching and learning far more than he could ever have dreamed. Tim's background was in the field of tennis, both as a player and as a coach, and in this work he became fascinated with the conversations that players would have with themselves on the court.

He noticed that many of them were actually giving themselves instructions out loud, and indeed he comments in his book that for some of them it was like hearing a recording of the last session playing inside their head. When he asked the players who they were talking to many would just say 'I'm actually talking to myself', but that then raised his curiosity further to ask the question who is this 'I' and who is 'myself'? It was logical for Tim to conclude that the two were treated as separate entities thus enabling the conversation. By way of simplifying this he referred to the 'I' as self 1 and the 'myself' as self 2, self 1 being the person who tells the body what to do and self 2 being the person that carries out the activity. As an astute observer and player of the game, Tim also noticed that self 1 very often had derogatory comments about self 2's performance. In many training textbooks this is often referred to as people being harder on themselves than anyone else could be. This misunderstanding has led to many cases of incompetence and not managing performance by many of today's managers and team leaders in the workplace. Tim builds on this by relating to the relationship between self 1 and self 2 as a way to improve performance. He does this by improving the relationship between the two. This fascinating insight is brought home even further when, as Tim suggests, we think of self 1 and self 2, not as parts of the same person, but as two completely separate people.

Since Tim's work, further areas of coaching have been developed in a non-directive manner, many of which have been brought over from the field of counselling and all with the aim of developing better performance. I think it is fair to point out that non-directive coaching should be put in the context of what is being called for by self 2; for example, if self 2 is calling for instructions and guidance and self 1, or any other person, refuses to give instruction or insists on taking a non-directive approach, this can just cause interference. It would not be the first time an individual has been heard to say to a colleague, 'I wish he would just tell me what to do instead of trying this coaching stuff'.

In Tim's later book *The Inner Game of Work* (2002), he talks about the three corners of a triangle as awareness, choice and trust (ACT) and self 2 focus. Having a greater understanding of these can help us improve the relationship between self 1 and self 2. Under the category of 'awareness: the light of focused attention', he uses the metaphor of a spotlight to bring focus to objects, to give greater definition, clarity and dimensionality.

I once worked with an art teacher for a number of years and can recall how he used to split a blank canvas up into grids with pencil marks and then draw each grid separately, joining the grids up at a later date. Putting the canvas under this sort of microscope means it is given the right degree of attention and enables the fine points of the subject to be rendered in much greater detail than would otherwise have been possible. It was interesting to note that the artists themselves would very often acquire a greater understanding of the subject.

I also remember with curiosity how the art teacher would ask each student to go and stand at the back of the room to view their canvas from a distance to see if all of the grids were joining up once they had been filled in. There was usually a supply of pencil rubbers on the way back to the canvas as the student had focused so much on one grid that they had got it out of all proportion with the rest of the canvas, although that grid on its own was an absolute masterpiece.

The lesson here is to improve one's quality of attention and awareness, but to keep it in perspective. In a coaching context this means listening to what the client is saying but having the ability to stand to one side and see the bigger picture of the workplace. One of my clients once commented that the art of good coaching is not to charge in and sort them out when the client is 'too far into the woods to see the trees', it's to actually pull the client 'out of the woods' so they can see what they are doing.

In the second part of his book Tim goes on to talk about choice and focus, kicking off with a fundamental statement regarding this in terms of focus being governed by desire. He points out that a person connected with his desire notices the critical success factors. Indeed, I have seen this on many occasions where the self-determination of a footballer running towards the goal or a rugby player running towards the touchline is governed by desire and that desire can be fuelled very often by the crowd. It is of course our choice whether we are actually governed by desire, and we can chose which desires we want to go for and which ones we wish to ignore. In the context of the inner game we have a choice between listening to self 1 or not listening to self 1, encouraging self 2 or not encouraging self 2.

Steven Covey (2004) recalls that, in his time in a concentration camp in the Second World War, Victor Frankle had the choice of allowing the guards to influence his thinking or not. While a somewhat extreme example, Victor Frankle's teachings have gone on to become an inspiration for many as he had that same self-determination not to be influenced by his captors that many top sports people have in trying to realise the ultimate achievements in their field.

The last area of the triangle is trust and it is trust in self 2, the doer of the activity, that is crucial in this particular respect. Self 1 very often knocks self 2 and therefore would indicate that there is no trust at all as self 1 would lead you believe that he/she knows better. When self 2 actually carries out the action with a degree of spontaneity, something usually happens that is unexpected. Mihaly Csikszentmihalyi describes this in his book on the psychology of happiness as 'flow' (1992). He maintains that everyone experiences flow from time to time and will recognise its characteristics. People typically feel strong, wide-awake, in control, non-conspicuous and at the height of their performance, and many of their emotional problems appear to have vanished. It is important to note that this is not about dumbing down, but it is about getting into the flow and is not controlled by any one factor. Very often, as Tim pointed out, it takes trust and a bit of humility, the latter being an important part of focus and trust. On the journey to becoming a professional coach it is very easy to observe the arrogance that is around in the industry that has been brought over from the field of consulting. It actually serves the coach well to admit that they don't know everything that is going on as it gives them an insatiable desire to seek out the answers which the client can then learn from. There is a great deal of satisfaction from coaching somebody when they themselves come up with their own answers and have what one of my clients calls an 'Osram' moment when the light comes on for them.

From the point of view of the coach it is crucial to be at one with yourself before you actually start work with the client and the work of the inner game is one way of actually doing that. Where is your greatest source of interference? When do these interferences occur? What sort of nerves do you get prior to a coaching session? What is going through your mind in the middle of a coaching session? What interferes with seeing the actions through when you are following up on a coaching session? The answer to these questions will give you an indication as to what interference is actually acting upon you. Self 1 in this particular case is actually in the driving seat and is being pulled and pushed and therefore is putting pressure on self 2.

The best coaches have the focus and the determination to actually see things through right to the end. Very often in the workplace people have said to me that they haven't got time for soft, fluffy coaching stuff. However, as I have pointed out on many occasions, coaching is about hard and fast conversations. These hard and fast conversations can be facilitated best by self 2, that is the person that rolls up their sleeves and gets on and does the job, but they do the job of the coach, they don't do the job of the client and doing the job of the coach is about having the degree of focus throughout the entire conversation that facilitates concrete actions that will be checked up on by both the individual and the coach at the next session. This then leads us to believe that the influence of self 1 is prompted by one's own actions. Should you fail to follow up on a previous coaching session, this will almost certainly play on your mind and cause doubt when you come to prepare for the next coaching session. You may know that the client will ask questions, even in their own mind even if they are not brave enough to ask you out loud.

Developing relationships

Relationships occur in everyday life, whether at work, at play, socially or in a sports environment. We have a relationship with everyone that we meet – we might not always be aware of it but we do. However, the kind of relationship that we would look at in a coaching partnership is based upon the goals of both the client and the coach. So there is a shared commitment that is involved here, whereas in many relationships there is a pull either one way or the other. In some cases coaching actually fails because the client does not share the commitment or there is an imbalance between the commitment of the two parties. It is not an uncommon phenomenon to see a very enthusiastic committed coach and, because of the appointment through a third party, either an HR department or the client's manager, an apathetic client. It is the view of many coaches that if the shared commitment is not present the coaching cannot take place in its current manner. However, this provides a wonderful opportunity for the coach to actually use as a call for action. By following the client's train of thought the coach can find out what the client is committed to and use that as a starting place. James Flaherty, in *Coaching – Evoking Excellence in Others* (1999), regards the elements of the coaching relationship as mutual trust, mutual respect and mutual freedom of expression, and these three elements bring together the dynamic of the coaching relationship. He uses the word mutual to indicate that it is a partnership between both the client and the coach.

Mutual trust

Mutual trust is an interesting concept. It is one of these things that we know when it is not there, but it is taken for granted when it is there. It is a good coaching question to ask a client, 'How do you know when you actually trust someone?' Further questions along this theme are: 'How did you arrive at trusting this individual?' 'How is trust repaired when it is broken?' 'Is there a choice over who we trust?' 'Is it a choice that we are aware of?' These questions can be extremely useful when working with an individual in an attempt to repair relationships in the workplace, so you may wish to make a note of them and add them to your battery of questions for future use. Steven Covey talks extensively in *The Seven Habits of Highly Effective People* (2004) about the elements of trust and trustworthiness and the relationship between the two. Covey points out that trust comes from trustworthiness and individuals have a responsibility to be trustworthy. The situation is no different for the coach. A trustworthy coach will develop trust in a relationship. My own point of view is that trustworthiness comes from a degree of transparency and integrity. To put it another way, trustworthiness comes from being authentic, being the real you. In the film *The Legend of Bagger Vance*, Bagger (Will Smith) is trying to enable golfer Rannulph Junuh (Matt Damon) to find his 'authentic swing', that is the swing that is inherently his, that belongs to no one else and comes from the real Junuh. As a coach if we can allow clients to see the authentic us, the real us, we can develop our part of the partnership that is mutual trust. However, there would need to be some work done on the client's part and this is very often facilitated by the coach. The key component is, as far as the client is concerned, based around the presupposition that we trust people because we make up our minds to do so and not because we are forced into it. So it is about you the coach creating the right environment, the right climate and the right conditions that make you trustworthy. We can't make up our client's mind for them. They have to make their own mind up, based upon what they see, feel and hear.

From your point of view then let's determine what it is we trust about you, the coach. It is very rare in life to trust absolutely everybody for everything all of the time. So breaking the question down a little bit further, let's have a look at you, the coach, by asking if you are sincere in what you say. Are you transparent? Do you keep your promises? Are you consistent with the same person and with different people? To use Steven Covey's words again, 'If you want to maintain the trust of those present, be loyal to those that are absent' (Covey, 2004).

The second aspect of trust actually comes from the individual's level of competence, so let's have a look at yourself as a coach in this area. Have you demonstrated competence as a coach? You can check this against the associated behaviours that are listed for the ten core competencies in Appendix 2. To use a slightly different analogy in terms of competency, think about yourself as a passenger in a vehicle. Think about yourself when driving with a competent driver and then think about yourself when, as a passenger, you are driving with, in your words, an incompetent driver. There are some clear distinctions to be made between competence here. How do you feel? What is going through your mind? What is the trustworthiness rating of the driver that is competent and the one that is incompetent? The same thing applies and will be put into practice by clients when working with you once they have assessed your degree of competence. The final point with regard to the mutual trust aspect is that it needs to be held in context and the context that we are looking at here is that the coach needs to be trustworthy and the coach needs to have that feeling of trustworthiness among their clients in the coaching relationship.

Mutual respect

The word 'respect' is going through a reformation and has been doing so over the past ten years or so as a standard greeting among young people. It is encouraging to see this happening. However, many people say that respect needs to be earned and this is also an interesting concept. Do we work for it as we work for reward? Do we collect it like a series of certificates of competence as when we progress through sports and social activities at school? Or do we fight for it like earning your stripes in the armed forces? The very essence of respect is about accepting an individual for what they are – in this particular case your client. Once again James Flaherty (1999) maintains that respect is based upon a spectrum with, at one end, mild acceptance and, at the other, total admiration. At the acceptance end, he maintains that it's the values and behaviour of someone that is what we find to be tolerable. On the admiration side it's not only about tolerance, it's about fully endorsing their values and behaviour when we hold them up as a model for ourselves and others.

It is easy to see how mutual respect forms the basis of the coaching relationship. The coach needs to respect the client in that they want to develop themselves, move on and progress, and the client certainly needs to respect the coach for what they can actually bring to the relationship. However, sometimes that client has expectations of a different nature. Their misunderstanding is that the coach is going to tell them what to do or, even worse, do it for them. This needs to be clarified at the very outset in the contracting stage by determining what the coaching style is going to be.

From the coach's point of view, when they are deciding whether they respect someone or not they make a value judgement as to whether or not the potential client could be coached by them. It maybe that you need to take up the conversation again to establish more about the potential client.

It is not too dissimilar to the aspect of trust, especially when looking at past behaviour. The coach needs to distinguish what has happened in the past from an objective point of view from what other people thought or felt had happened. This is an important point because unless the coach separates out what has actually happened from what other people have thought or felt has happened, they will become tied up with clients that they are closely aligned to, in other words clients who they like or feel comfortable with.

I remember in a previous company consultants used to work with organisational clients at a substantially lower rate, justifying this by saying that they needed to get inside the organisation to facilitate change from within rather than approach it from outside. If you actually looked at this in the cold light of day you would see that the consultant was so aligned with the client that it was comfortable for them to work there.

Thus one of the ways that respect can actually be earned is by putting yourself in situations, not where you are laying yourself open to the charge of incompetence, but where you are continually developing yourself through working in arenas that are tough, hard and sometimes uncompromising. It is an important distinction to make that mutual respect does not come about just because someone is 'like me'; it comes down to a judgement we make. Therefore it is a choice, but that choice needs to be objective, prudent and conducted with due diligence. Look at what has happened in the past and make a clinical decision by asking the question: 'What would this relationship be like if I respect this person?' Then compare this with the similar question: 'What would this relationship be like if I don't respect this person?' The context in which you are asking this is what the outcome will be to your shared commitment and the relationship with your client.

Mutual freedom of expression

The third and final part of the coaching relationship comes down to mutual freedom of expression and as it is the third and final part it builds on its two predecessors. A basic understanding of what we mean by mutual freedom of expression is needed here. The common conception is that people can say whatever they want, however they want to say it, whenever they want and to whomever they want, and in many cases this is absolutely right. The old argument regarding leadership comes to mind here – that is anyone can lead, but will others follow? In this particular case anybody can say whatever they want, to whomever they want, whenever they want, however they want to, but will others listen?

First and foremost the coach has to build freedom of expression into the relationship – it is not to be taken for granted. This is about setting the right conditions where the coach invites the client to speak openly and positions himself to give the free attention that is referred to in John Heron's 'Catalytic Toolkit'. Doing this constructs the platform for the freedom of expression to exist, live and thrive. It also builds on the transparency that was referred to earlier. There is nothing hidden and both coach and client are quite prepared to contribute freely as part of the mutual relationship. The key factor in this is the listening, and in this sense this means not just engaging your ears and the auditory nerves, it is the full engagement of attention, thought and intention of the coach. The Chinese symbol 'to listen' (see Figure 3.1) invites the listener to use their ears

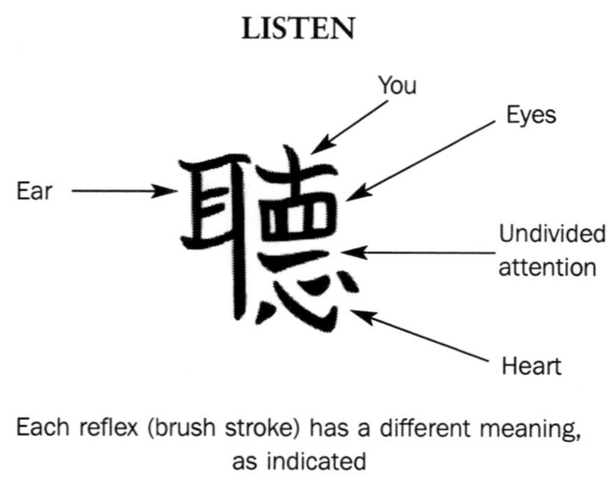
LISTEN
You
Eyes
Ear
Undivided attention
Heart
Each reflex (brush stroke) has a different meaning, as indicated

Figure 3.1 The Chinese character 'to listen'.

and their eyes, to focus on the person they are listening to, to give their undivided attention and their heart, and it is all of these faculties that actually brings out true listening. Flaherty (1999) maintains that the combination of the three elements – openness, listening and confidentiality – will ensure freedom of expression in the coaching relationship.

Aileen Gibb and the team at I.C. International, who strive tirelessly to bring soul back to the world of work to act as coach and conscience, pay particular attention to the coaching relationship and these three areas of mutual trust, mutual respect and mutual freedom of expression. They all challenge with integrity if one of these three elements is missing from any business transaction that they engage in with any of their clients, colleagues or associates. A key component of this is down to the listening that they employ.

One of Aileen's guiding principles is that listening is respect in action and that is the staring point for the whole team at I.C. International. They will develop their listening and bring it to play on mutual trust, mutual respect and mutual freedom of expression. They have a tendency to objectively review those three elements and come back to you if there are any undue concerns, not only on their part, but if they are sensing them on yours also. The relationship is the foundation for excellent coaching and it is important that those foundations are solid. On the journey of coaching there will be many mistakes and if the foundations are unsure then the demise of the coaching will soon follow. Relationship is also about investment and a good firm investment in the relationship that you develop as a coach will stand you in good stead for the future. You must continually strive to strengthen these three elements of trust, respect and freedom of expression.

The four pillars of trust

A key factor in our ability to connect effectively with others is our perceived accessibility. Unfortunately, the accelerated pace of the contemporary workplace leaves too many people feeling frustrated and devalued following interactions with managers and colleagues.

Though you may not be able to control the quantity of time you have available to interact with others, you can control the quality of that time.

This model takes into account the presence of the coach and the approach that the coach needs to adopt when coaching. This requires a technique of questioning that has no bias to it and a commitment to making the process work. These four pillars, as illustrated in Figure 3.2, bring together the trusting partnership that makes up the coach's way of being.

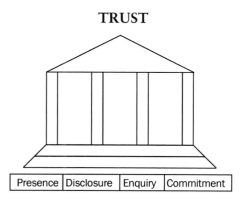

Figure 3.2 The four pillars of trust.

The model outlines the main elements of effective interaction with others, provides a diagnostic tool to allow participants to establish how they respond to people and situations, and introduces techniques that may be used to increase the levels of trust and partnership with others.

The four pillars of trust

Presence: Bringing an authentic self to one's interactions with others and sustaining a high degree of focus, energy and openness towards others.

The quality of attention that a coach brings to others is an essential part of building a trusting relationship. Truly 'being present' for someone takes time and effort, but when you demonstrate the gift of your presence, you communicate just how important something is to you.

Three critical factors determine to a great extent the presence a coach is able to muster and maintain in any given interaction with others. These factors are:

1. *Focus* – the attention the coach brings to the moment.

2. *Openness* – the receptivity of heart and mind the coach brings to the moment.

3. *Energy* – the physical and emotional vigour the coach brings to the moment.

Disclosure: Accurate, timely and candid sharing of personal thoughts and feelings and organisational information that can, or does, impact on performance and working relationships.

Enquiry: The disposition to seek after another's perspective, stemming from a recognition and acknowledgement of the other as a source of value, wisdom, insight and unique experience.

Commitment: Consistency and reliability of follow-through as demonstrated by the fulfilment of promises made to others.

Focus, openness and energy – an assessment tool

The diagnostic tool shown in Figure 3.3 may be used in a number of situations:

RIGHT NOW	LEVEL: 1 (lowest) – 10 (highest)
Focus	
Openness	
Energy	
Total	

Adapted from Cooper and Sawaf (1996).

Figure 3.3 The FOE assessment tool

- *As a self-assessment tool.* With awareness comes the ability to adapt accordingly and to understand more clearly what is behind one's own reactions to people and situations.

- *As an assessment of the other.* Asking these three questions of the person you coach may help you to decide to what extent the time is right for instruction and learning, for problem-solving or for delivering feedback.

- *As a team tool.* You can use this tool with teams at the beginning of meetings to enhance awareness, to acknowledge differences and to prevent many common misinterpretations of behaviour.

Six presence killers

Listed below are a number of scenarios that are commonplace in a work situation and result in ineffective interactions. Pragmatic verbal and non-verbal solutions are offered to address the negative impact of these exchanges:

- assuming the exit position – giving the impression you are ready to leave;

- offering 'only' time – using expressions such as 'I can only spare five minutes';

- two timing – not being honest with your client;

- the democracy of interruptions – taking mobile/cell phone calls;

- pseudo-presence – trying to give the impression that you are there and/or listening;

- filtering – listening for specific areas that give you an opportunity to interrupt, i.e. 'listening for' rather than 'listening to'.

> 'Coaching is an art, not a science. Not a technique, but a way of being, an orientation towards others.'
>
> Ken Blanchard

Further reading

The preparation of the coach

Whyte, David (1994) *The Heart Aroused.* Currency Doubleday.
Whyte, David (2001) *Crossing the Unknown Sea.* Michael Joseph.

The coaching contract

Hargrove, Robert (1995) *Masterful Coaching.* Pfeiffer Wiley.

The inner game

Gallwey, Tim (1986) *The Inner Game of Tennis.* Pan.
Gallwey, Tim (2002) *The Inner Game of Work.* Texere Publishing.

Csikszentmihalyi, Mihaly (1992) *Flow – The Psychology of Happiness*. Rider.

Covey, Stephen (2004) *The Seven Habits of Highly Effective People*. Simon & Schuster.

Developing relationships

Covey, Stephen (2004) *The Seven Habits of Effective People*. Simon & Schuster.

Flaherty, James (1999) *Coaching – Evoking Excellence in Others*. Butterworth-Heinemann.

The Legend of Bagger Vance (2000). 20th Century Fox (DVD).

Further information

Jim Laughlin is a consultant who works for Linkage International and has developed a great deal of material in the field of coaching. He may be contacted as follows:

Jim Laughlin, Linkage International, 1 Forbes Road, Lexington, MA 02173, USA.

4

Maintaining the coaching

The GROW model

The GROW model is one methodology used by performance coaches to guide their approach to the coaching session and maximise their effectiveness. The aim of performance coaching is to raise the client's awareness and responsibility. The GROW model includes techniques that may be applied by the coach to achieve these objectives. In summary the purpose of the GROW model is to:

- compel attention;
- focus on precision and detail; and
- create a feedback loop.

There are five steps to using this model (see Figure 4.1). The first step is to identify the topic that the client wants to be coached on. This is usually quite a large subject and the coach needs to enable the client to get more specific about the topic. Once this has happened the main process, often referred to by the four-letter acronym GROW, involves the coach establishing the following from the client:

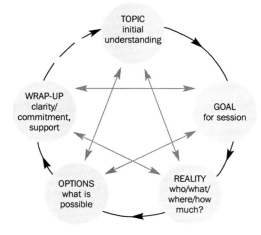

Reproduced by kind permission of Myles Downey.

Figure 4.1 The GROW model.

- Goals - What do you want?
- Reality – What is happening now?
- Options – What could you do?
- Wrap up, way forward and will – What will you do?

Goal

The *goal* is established at the beginning of the session, for the session, by the client. It touches on the topic that will be covered during the period of the coaching session. It is therefore important to ensure that the goal is a realistic one for the duration of the session time available.

Once established, *write the goal down*. It can then be used throughout the coaching session to review progress and to instil confidence in the client. It is also prudent to summarise and pull the goal into the summary at the end of the session.

It is important for the coach to prepare for this initial session by ensuring that he or she has the most effective mind-set for the coaching session. This can be achieved by examining their FOE factors:

- Focus
- Openness
- Energy.

These critical factors determine to a great extent the presence a coach is able to muster and maintain in any given interaction with others:

1. *Focus* – is the attention the coach has for their client and to the moment.
2. *Openness* – is how receptive, in a non-judgemental manner, the coach is to the content of what is being said.
3. *Energy* – is the degree to which the coach is 'up for it', both mentally and physically.

A coach can rate themselves on a scale of 1–10 for each area (FOE). A low score indicates that you are 'your own worst enemy'.

Reality

The concept of *reality* in the GROW model is to facilitate an awareness to perceive things as they really are – self-awareness is recognising those internal factors that distort one's own perception of reality. Absolute objectivity is impossible, but we can achieve a variety of perceptions that give us a more complete picture. This session requires detachment on the part of the coach and factual answers and statements from the client.

The fundamental principle on which this session is based is that problems or issues must be addressed at the level beneath that at which they show themselves if they are to be permanently eliminated. In order for this to happen there must be an appreciation of the current reality from as many perspectives as possible. Accordingly the reality session in GROW is for the benefit of the client and not the coach. It is the raising of self-awareness in this stage that allows for the cause rather than just the effect to be dealt with.

Options

The purpose of the *options* stage of GROW is to create and list as many alternative courses of actions as possible. It is this stage in the process that will determine how successful the 'way forward' stage will be.

It is crucial during this stage that the coach creates an environment where the client feels safe enough to express all thoughts and ideas without fear of judgement. Once the coach and client have exhausted all possibilities the coach then reflects back the options and explores the possibilities with the client. The use of a benefit/drawback grid (see Figure 4.2) may assist in drawing out pertinent issues in relation to the options, including practicalities, cost, quality, time, etc. On concluding this exercise, sufficient objective

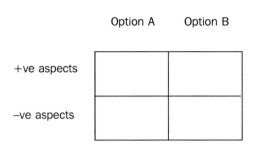

Fill in the boxes with the positive and negative
aspects of each option.

Figure 4.2 Benefit/drawback grid

information will be available to make a responsible
decision.

Way forward and wrap-up

This final stage of the GROW model facilitates the *way
forward* for the client and ultimately leads to a decision and
the construction of an action plan. This stage adds the finer
detail of the primary choice arising out of the options stage.
The goal of the coach is to ensure that the session leads to
clarity, commitment and a sense of purpose on the part of
the client and accordingly requires the coach to take a
pragmatic approach to the session, reflecting on any
potential problems that have arisen previously.

> 'It is the construction of an action plan to meet a
> requirement that has been clearly specified, on a ground
> that has been thoroughly surveyed, using the widest
> possible choice of building materials.'
>
> Sir John Whitmore

The coaching spectrum and the suggestion map

The coaching spectrum

As can be seen from Figure 4.3, the coaching spectrum involves a range of approaches to conversations with a client. At one end of the spectrum we have 'directive', which is pushing and solving someone's problem for them, through the range to 'non-directive', which is pulling and helping someone solve their own problem. There is no doubt that the most effective end of the spectrum to work at is the non-directive as you are working with the client's own map of reality and their own understanding of procedures and processes. However, having said that, it is probably the most

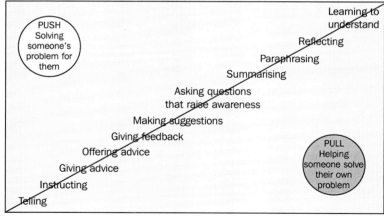

Reproduced by kind permission of Myles Downey.

Figure 4.3 The coaching spectrum

difficult end to work at, especially if one knows the subject extremely well. It is inherent in each of us to prefer to tell someone what to do, rather than ask questions and let them tell you what they think. The following notes give some understanding as to each of the levels on the spectrum.

Telling

This is the end of the spectrum that we are most familiar with. From the instructions that we learnt as a child when we were told by our parents, or from the way that we were educated when we were told in school, this is a habit subject to social conditioning that we find very hard to break out of. One way in which you might contemplate breaking the habit is to consider how you feel when you are told something:

- Do you do exactly as you are told?
- Do you resent being told?
- Do you listen when you are told something?
- Do you challenge any misunderstanding when you are told something, or do you just accept it and do your own thing anyway?

Answering some of these questions could give you some insight into how effective the telling really is.

Instructing

There is no doubt that each of us learn in different ways. We store information differently and the way that we access it once it is stored is also different. Both of these areas need to be considered when we are working with giving instructions. Through life experience people have a general understanding of anything they are going to do anyway and it is this platform that needs to be considered when giving instructions. Asking questions – for example, 'What do you know about it already?' or 'Have you approached it before?' – helps to ensure that the instructions are received and understood. Any instructions need to be placed in the context of what needs to be taught and the context of what the learner already knows. If we add to this an understanding of the practical learning styles mentioned above it can make a big difference.

Giving advice

This is usually a tricky one as giving advice normally masquerades as 'telling'. We try to soften the telling so it becomes more advisory rather than dogmatic in its approach. Once again consider what advice needs to be received by the person, what context do they need to see this advice in, what are they going to do with the advice once they have received it, and does this advice contradict any advice previously received? All of these areas need to be considered if we are going to give advice effectively.

Offering guidance

If giving advice is a watered-down telling, then very often offering guidance is a watered-down giving advice. Offering guidance is usually positioned from the coach's previous experience – once again it is held in a context of past behaviour and conditions. One of the concerns that Sir John

Whitmore has about offering guidance is that very often you can be giving yesterday's solution to tomorrow's problem. The way to combat this is to ask how the client is going to use the guidance, not whether they have received it. In addition, asking what the consequences are of using the guidance in such a way can help to ensure that the client feels that they have something of real value once the guidance has been given.

Giving feedback

Feedback is certainly one of the most useful aspects of coaching, and if given properly it is the one that the client can derive the most benefit from. However, we need to consider what giving feedback properly really means. First and foremost feedback has to be accurate. There are no prizes for second-guessing when giving feedback – it can damage the relationship, the trust and your reputation as a coach. So ensure that the feedback that you are about to give is accurate. Secondly, feedback has to be useful; that is to say, will the client be able to use the information that you are giving them? Although this seems rather an obvious point, ask yourself the question, ' If the client gets upset by what you say, or disputes what you say, how likely is it that they are going to use it?' Considering these two thoughts before we start can help us couch feedback in such a way that it can be received and be beneficial to the client.

Making suggestions

At this stage we are about half way through the spectrum so when making suggestions we should start to look at how we can actually do so in the client's map of reality. One of the ways of doing this is to use a suggestion map (see p. 104). When someone asks you if you have any suggestions, it is not always clear in what context they are looking for the suggestions to be made. One way of solving this is to write down all of the possibilities, giving your past experience of suggested ways forward and talking through a little bit of the context as you do it. At this point you can then ask the client which one of those 'ways forward' is most in accord with what they are currently thinking. Once they have pointed out which one you can then have a further discussion in that area.

Asking questions that raise awareness

Asking questions is the key tool that the coach has in the toolbox of coaching skills. The classic – who, what, where, when and how – are all extremely beneficial questions that will generally raise the awareness of the client. Asking the 'why' question could also raise the awareness of the client, but it tends to be somewhat confrontational as the client generally responds with an answer that involves some justification on their part and can put them under pressure. So while you may have raised awareness, you may also have closed down the conversation slightly. On many of the courses we run we use little dice with Who, What, Where, When, How and the Chinese symbol to listen printed on the six sides. Using the coaching dice can help you break any habits you might have, such as batching questions or asking closed questions. (These dice can be purchased by contacting the author.)

Summarising

Moving closer to the non-directive end of the spectrum, summarising has many benefits. Firstly, if we summarise accurately it can indicate to the client that we have been listening. Secondly, summarising is a standard way of reinforcing memory and retention. Summarising is best used at the end of a session as it can indicate closure before moving onto a new area.

Paraphrasing

Paraphrasing follows similar rules to summarising, except it is generally used in the session just to recap, clarify understanding and challenge any assumptions. Just as the paragraph is the written unit, so the paraphrase is the spoken unit.

Reflecting

Reflecting is best used by the coach to question past events through conversation with as opposed to questioning the client. Reflections are very often made up of hypothetical questions, for example:

- 'I was wondering what would have happened if we had made the deadline?'
- 'If the budget was larger, how would that have changed things?'

Reflections are a very useful way of maintaining a non-directive stance.

Listening to understand

Many people regard listening to understand as the coach listening so that the coach understands. While having some degree of accuracy, this is not the full concept of listening to understand. The idea is that the coach communicates with the client in such a way that the client then responds to the coach. During this response, the coach should create the right ambience and atmosphere to allow the client to contribute to the conversation in such a way that the client is actually listening to what they are saying themselves and in many cases understanding for the first time the full implication of the content of their response. This can only be done where there is exceptionally high trust, little interference and the right questions have been asked in the first instance.

The suggestion map

In the coaching spectrum discussed previously (see Figure 4.3) making suggestions appears in the middle, but there is a way to get it to the non-directive end of the scale for mutual benefit and greater impact.

The coach will often be asked 'What would you do?' That being so they need to make a judgement call regarding their next steps. Also, as much as the coach tries to remain non-judgemental, there is usually some interference in the form of their own ideas and suggestions. One way of addressing both these above scenarios is to use the suggestion map.

Whenever we are confronted with a blockage it is usually made up of more than one component. This is the key to the suggestion map.

Take a blank piece of paper and jot down all the aspects of the topic in hand randomly, not in a list. Once this has been done, making sure you have included the suggestion you were going to make or the one causing interference, turn the paper round and ask which one relates most to the concerns of your client. This then gives the client the opportunity to regain control of the conversation. It is not unusual for the client to point to the 'one word' from your map that works for them and ask for more information from the coach about it.

Consider, for example, a client who has asked for coaching in making a presentation, in particular to improve her confidence. She has reached a point in the coaching that goes along the following lines:

Client: As a coach you've had to make a lot of presenta-tions – how do you manage to appear so confident?

Coach: Well, my degree of confidence is built up from several areas, for example ... [the coach now drafts out Figure 4.4 then places the page in front of his client.] Which one of these gives you most anxiety?

Client: Actually, it's not on the sheet – well not directly anyway. There is new legislation just coming in and I'm not too sure of the impact it will have. I suppose it would come under subject knowledge.

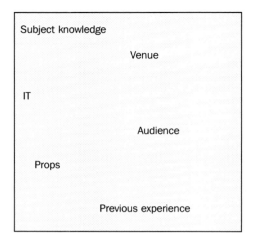

Figure 4.4 Suggestion map for coaching
in making a presentation.

Coach: So let's see if I've picked it up right. You have to make a presentation and you're not too confident about it.

Client: Right.

Coach: And upon probing further we find in the background that there is some new legislation coming in on the subject matter and you are anxious about the impact that this will have.

Client: Right.

Coach: Is there a link between this anxiety and your confidence?

Client: Yeah, I think there is – I'm afraid that someone will ask a question that I can't answer.

Coach: So if we work with this anxiety we should be able to get the confidence up. We might not be able to cover every eventuality regarding questions, but it will give you a good grounding.

Client: Yes I can see that.

From this example it can be seen that the suggestion map assisted the coach in finding the root cause. What followed was a conversation that was client-centred and client-led.

The suggestion map is a very useful tool in helping to eliminate other thoughts, distractions or interference that the coach might have. It can also help the coach in breaking the habit of 'telling'.

The skill/will matrix

The skill/will matrix (see Figure 4.5) has been further developed by Max Landsberg (1997) as a method of ensuring that a manager's or coach's style of interaction is matched to the client's readiness for a particular task. He suggests that one of the most likely reasons why a delegated task does not get completed satisfactorily is because the person undertaking the task may either be unwilling or unable to do so. Similarly, when coaching someone we can often 'feel' that something is not right with our approach or the client's receiving of the conversation. In this case it is worth looking at your style of interaction with the client's readiness for the challenge.

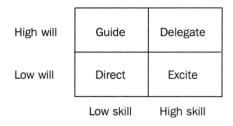

	Low skill	High skill
High will	Guide	Delegate
Low will	Direct	Excite

Figure 4.5 The skill/will matrix.

The skill/will matrix can assist in ensuring that the appropriate approach is adopted by the coach:

- First, diagnose the client's skill and will to accomplish the challenge, as indicated on the chart in Figure 4.5.

- Then use the matrix to identify the appropriate style of interaction, e.g. you would want to use 'Delegate' if the client was high in both skill and will.

- Finally, agree with your client which style you will be using and for what reasons. In his book *The Tao of Coaching* (1997), author Max Landsberg offers a few observations.

- Ensure that you are addressing the client's skill and will to execute the specific challenge in question, e.g. 'making presentations to the board of directors' rather than 'public speaking'.

- If you are working with someone over a long period, you will want them to increase in both skill and will. If they are successful in doing this you will need to gradually adopt the appropriate styles en route to 'delegate'.

- Skill depends upon experience, training, understanding and role perception.

- Will depends on the desire to achieve, incentives, security and confidence.

Application of the skill/will matrix

Direct (skill and will are both low)

This is an interesting area as you are dealing with someone who does not want to do something and does not know how to do it.

There needs to be a direct approach to this which involves working with the will first. This is the time for a hard direct conversation. It would not be the first time someone has asked the question 'What do you want to do?' only to be told 'I dunno!' Focus on the end goal first and build up the desire – only then can we get to grips with how we are going to get there.

Guide (low skill, high will)

I always relate this to working with graduate recruits in an organisation. They are as keen as mustard to get on. However, there is very little corporate skill in place. If many of the graduate recruits were left alone during the first weeks of their career, it would be over before it started. I find the following headings useful to get an idea of the type of guidance being called for.

- *People* – in this area a coach can give guidance on the type of people the client is working with, personal styles, preferences, etc.

- *Politics* – in this area a coach can highlight the cultural norms that happen in the corporate world and the 'games' that are being played out. This is also an area that a mentor can help in as they usually know the way of the corporate world.

- *Policies* – this is quite a good opportunity to get the client to go and find the policies on particular subjects and coach them on their interpretation using a model such as the four cornerstones.

- *Practices* – this heading can lead on from the previous one (policies) or stand alone. By establishing the policies first the client can then relate to the practices. Policies differ from practices in that the policy is what the manual says and the practice is what happens. On a stand-alone basis quite effective coaching sessions can occur as a result of asking what the client notices about the practice and then developing understanding further by challenging interpretation.

- *Activities* – this last heading relates to training to acquire a skill set rather than anything else. It is where I very often use referrals to others who are experts in the activity to train the individual.

Excite (high skill, low will)

In this area of the matrix it is important to remember that it is your approach we are referring to here. As such your approach should be one that the client would find exciting. For me this usually means taking the client outside of their usual working environment. In an executive coaching assignment it is usual for me to use museums, art galleries, monuments and in one case even the Royal Yacht *Britannia* moored at Leith Docks as a way of getting a client to engage their imagination. In the latter case we imagined that the project the client had to work on was the last royal cruise prior to decommissioning. On the bridge of the Yacht, my client spoke at length regarding how he would organise such a cruise – being an ex-Navy officer, he had no problem in doing this. It was a short step to transfer his approach to this project to his current work project during which he sailed through the blockages he had built up (no pun intended)!

Delegate (skill and will are both high)

This is, or would be, the easiest area of the matrix if only we didn't have such a problem with delegation! Once again it is your approach we need to address. What do you do when you delegate effectively? I find the following are useful requirements to point out:

- clear communication with the person being delegated to;
- clear objectives;
- clear parameters and remit of responsibility;
- clearly understood monitoring schedule;
- clear context for the rest of the team.

Think about how you might use these points in a situation where the skill and will are high.

Taking account of others' skill and will

The idea of the skill/will matrix is simple but it needs practice to apply it effectively. The overall concept is that you tailor your style of coaching to the skill and will of the person you are coaching, bearing in mind the task they are trying to accomplish. There are two main challenges. First you have really to diagnose the client's skill and will, without leaping to conclusions based on prejudice or accepting the client's frequent pretence to be 'high skill and high will' at everything. Secondly, you need to modify your coaching style as the client builds both skill and will. If you can think of a time in the past where you were coached, taught or instructed and it didn't work, I would suggest that it was because the approach that the coach, tutor or instructor adopted did not complement the position at which you were on the grid.

As a coach always ask the client the questions 'Do you want to do it?' and 'Do you know how to do it?' The answers to these questions will give you the client's position on the grid. Get agreement from the client that that is where they are and then adopt the corresponding approach, i.e. if client was high will/low skill, the coach's approach should be to 'guide'. Enough reading – go try it out!

The STOP tool

In his book *The Inner Game of Work*, Tim Gallwey (2002) refers to self 1 as the character doing the talking and self 2 as the one who has to do the action. When self 1 is critical and dominant, it tends to interfere with self 2's innate ability to perform up to its potential. This is the basic framework from which the concept of the inner game seeks to overcome the interference and barriers that prevent us from achieving and exceeding our goals.

Tim argues that the hard part in the workplace is to remain aware while working. He maintains that it is important to us not only to achieve our goals on time, but to achieve them in a way that is satisfying. He adds to this that it is also important to enjoy and learn while accomplishing the task at hand. He concludes the opening part of his argument by maintaining that the various pressures, routines and momentums of our daily work life make it difficult to remain truly conscious.

He builds on his argument by entering into the domain of performance momentum. He defines this as a kind of activity that most of us are familiar with but is not done with conscious intent or awareness of purpose. In other words, he is talking about those habitual actions that we do in the course of a day without a moment's thought for why we do them. He maintains that it is fair comment that many routines that humans perform do not require one to be conscious, and often it is a relief not to give them conscious attention, almost like a default mode. From a learning perspective it is this default mode that actually causes the problem. The majority of learning is taken in through the conscious mind and not the subconscious and, as is illustrated above, it is the subconscious mind that is actually carrying out these activities.

The idea behind the STOP tool is to enable an individual to step outside the subconscious activities that they are performing and to review them with a degree of conscious awareness that will allow for improvement, understanding and progression. I can remember in an earlier career as a restaurant manager there were certain peak times throughout the course of the day when everybody was at their work stations and the object of the exercise was to provide quality, service and cleanliness, but also to 'fill the till'. The manager's role during this particular time was purely to motivate staff, keep an eye on customer service levels, keep an eye on quality and to ensure the smooth running of the restaurant. However, it was usually during these times that financial records were broken, either by producing consecutive back-to-back hours of record sales through the tills or through one particular peak rush.

A typical example of this was an annual firework display that was held outside one restaurant at Milton Keynes. Every year they consistently broke the record of the previous year and the whole restaurant would gear themselves up, as would the company, for this particular record-breaking event. On one such occasion the management team and I stepped outside the restaurant to have a look at the firework display and on turning round to come back into the restaurant we noticed numerous things that we would not have otherwise seen had we remained on site. Having stepped back from the operation we now had the opportunity to think about what we were going to do to ensure we were ready for the next rush after the firework display was over. We took ten minutes once back inside the restaurant to organise our thoughts and then each of us proceeded with our own work plans. I now realise that this was what Tim Gallwey referred to as the STOP tool:

- Step back
- Think
- Organise your thoughts and
- Proceed.

Step back

It is a very short step for us to actually take this into the art of coaching itself. The first part is to step back. The coach here needs to create the right environment and engage in the right kind of dialogue that allows the client to put some degree of distance between themselves and the particular activity that they are trying to get to grips with. They need to do this on a practical level, a physical level and a mental level. It is almost like creating space, not as a result of frustration but as a cognitive process with heightened awareness that will enable the individual to move through the model. A STOP can be of any duration and a good example of a short STOP would be the use of the FOE factors (see p. 88) prior to a coaching session to enable the coach to get in the right mindset for the coaching session itself.

Think

The next stage is to think. From experience, the way I have worked this with clients in the past is to arrange a series of questions that are not unlike the four cornerstones that allow an individual to develop a greater understanding and awareness of where they currently are. Some such questions include:

- What is the real objective?
- What is the intended end result?
- What is the purpose?
- Is there an agenda being followed – whose agenda?
- What are our priorities?
- Which direction would be best to follow?
- How can we define the issue more clearly?
- What are the consequences/impacts of such actions?
- What is missing?
- How would the customer see this issue?
- What is it that I really want?
- Are there any assumptions I am making?
- What do I know about my approach to the situation?

These are just some of the questions you could ask that would facilitate the thinking process that is required after you have stepped back from the particular issue. My favourite question here which always gets people thinking is: 'And what have I forgotten?' The use of these questions cannot help but place you in a conscious state of mind.

Organise your thoughts

Now we come to the point where the organisation of these thoughts, i.e. the answers to the questions, will enable us to get some kind of plan. One of the ways I have done this in the past is through using a classic brainstorming technique during the thinking process. Once the results of the brainstorming session are actually laid out on paper in front of the client, I then ask them to categorise them into similar areas using coloured pens and circling round similarities. Once we have got to this stage we can then start to put some logical order together that can be followed by both the client and their team. From a coaching perspective it is important to remember that the logical order should be the client's logical order, not the coach's logical order!

Proceed

The final part of the tool is proceed and this is where the client will actually roll their sleeves up and get back to work, or if you are the coach this is the point where you facilitate the client in listing the actual, practical actions that they will do to achieve the outcomes of the thinking process previously mentioned.

In *The Inner Game of Work* Tim Gallwey refers to the fact that you can have STOPs of different lengths. An example of a short STOP might be walking to the water cooler to get a glass of water or making a cup of coffee if you are at home. A medium STOP might be taking a walk outside to get a breath of fresh air and different perspective on things. In an example cited in *The Inner Game of Work* Tim relates the story of a colleague who went on a retreat at a monastery, which he referred to as a long STOP.

Tim also gives some advice on when to use STOPs, such as the beginning and close of each work day at which time you can actually look at what you will be doing and what it is you have done. On many time management courses they advocate putting together your action plan for the following day at the end of the previous day. This would be a typical example. Another illustration that Tim gives is to stop at the beginning and at the end of any work project. What is interesting about this is that in reality most project evaluations are usually left to the last minute and rushed through, so there is merit in using a STOP tool for this approach.

A third example that Tim provides is making a conscious change. This works particularly well when used with the four cornerstones model (see p. 32) and the STOP tool is used to ask questions in the four areas of history, big picture, consequences and assumptions. Once again he points out that it can be a short STOP, just to make some minor adjustments to the project or change, or a significant STOP which would usually be termed a review. Some of the questions regarding the conscious change STOP are:

- What has caused this change?
- What are the effects of this change?
- What are the real benefits?
- What are the real costs?
- Who is involved?
- What other changes are going on elsewhere?

- What have we done before that can influence this change?
- What have we done before that we can learn from this change?
- What is the communication necessary to facilitate this change?

The fourth area Tim suggests for the use of the STOP tool is to address mistakes. This particularly useful when used with young children as there is a series of questions, as already illustrated, that can help the child understand the context in which any mistakes occur. In addition, it helps them understand the bigger picture and the future implications of such mistakes. I know from working with my own children the benefit of actually getting them to STOP and step outside of what it is they are currently doing, asking them what they see, what it is they are trying to achieve and what it is that is blocking that achievement. I also know from working with my own children that it is extremely difficult as a parent to get the right approach first time and therefore the STOP tool could be used by the parent before working with the child.

The fifth area that Tim recommended is stopping to correct miscommunication. In particular he looks at two areas: speaking and listening. Under the speaking category, once you have facilitated the STOP, a series of questions will again help you connect with what it is you want to do, for example:

- What is it I really want to say?
- Is everything about me saying what I really want to say?

- What communication is needed – my thoughts, my feelings, my opinions, the facts, my feedback?
- What assumptions have I made in order to speak? (Such points are equally valid under the listening category.)
- What am I listening to?
- What am I listening for?
- What is the real message in what I am hearing?
- What is the response that is called for?
- What is the response that is appropriate?
- What is the response that I feel I should say?

The final usage of the STOP tool advocated by Tim is STOP to learn or to coach. Given what was said earlier in the book about understanding practical learning styles, a STOP to reflect on orientation, interaction, representation or processing is certainly beneficial. Once again, from experience, I know that the reflective parts of a training course are usually the bits that are actually missed out. This may be due to the trainer feeling uncomfortable with the silence or, due to a lack of time, reflection just before lunch or just before the close of play is missed out because the trainer has spent too much time trying to ram information into the delegates. Therefore I would recommend the inclusion of learning STOPs throughout any training programme, and the same goes for coaching. A useful statement for the coach to make is: 'Let's just take five minutes to reflect on where the learning is on what we have done so far.' This can then be followed up with the question: 'What are the implications for your own project or job?'

once the individual has stopped and reflected on the learning.

There is also a case, Tim points out, for taking a STOP just to rest. The objective is simply to rest and allow the body and the brain to rejuvenate, so there is nothing to think about or organise. He also suggests a change of posture, for example if you have been sitting down then get up and have a walk about, or, if you have been constantly on the move then take time just to sit down and relax and unwind. Quite a few organisations are now providing space for this in the workplace.

The final point Tim makes is the real objective of STOP, and that is to get going. While this sounds like a paradox in the way that the tool is used, it is almost like 'making time, to enable time to make'. And the warning shot across the bows is, as one would expect from Tim Gallwey, that if you let 'self 1' impose STOPs as a 'should' on you, you will miss the benefit that they can bring. Just go with the STOPs and don't analyse them to death.

Feedback

Feedback skills

Feedback is an integral component of two-way communication in the coaching process. It is the only indication that the message you intended to send has been received correctly. Feedback is also an effective tool for developing and reinforcing relationships. Breakdown in effective interaction is often a result of lack of appropriate feedback.

This section looks at giving feedback after instructional skills or coaching and giving feedback in the workplace. It looks at feedback and how to position it so that offence is not taken and it can be of use to the recipient.

Ten golden rules for performance feedback

1. Find out what the client was trying to achieve.

2. Build a track record of responding to achievements and thereby earn the right to comment on performance weaknesses.

3. First consider the part you and the work environment play in the performance you observe.

4. Link your short-term coaching agenda to what is important to the person you are coaching.

5. Know when to abandon your agenda.

6. Ask individuals to assess their own performance first.

7. Focus on behaviour and consequences. Relate behaviour to its impact.

8. Allow the individual time to think and respond. Model thoughtful silence.

9. Avoid locking into one solution – define the expected result, but leave the specific route to attaining that result up to the individual.

10. Inquire and set the contract – for you to be successful as a coach, you must ask your client: 'What kind of coach do you need me to be?' Get some agreement on

the ground rules that you need to have about the way you give feedback. This is what is meant by 'setting the contract'.

Types of feedback

Feedback has to be useful (i.e. the client can make use of it) and it has to be accurate and balanced. Generally, there are two types of feedback: positive (praise) and negative (criticism).

1. *Positive feedback*. Most employees like and need regular feedback to know they are appreciated and are performing in an acceptable manner.
2. *Negative feedback*. This should be undertaken in an unemotional, objective and specific manner. It should be constructive in nature, outlining how the client may improve their behaviour.

Receiving negative feedback

It is very difficult to be the recipient of criticism and it is an experience that can trigger the urge to retaliate. Table 4.1 outlines a number of ways in which to appropriately deal with difficult responses in a coaching situation.

All the suggestions in Table 4.1 rely on three basic themes:

- If there's a problem in the conversation, *acknowledge it*.
- Be prepared for the agenda to shift from what you originally planned.

■ Be open to the possibility that things are not as you thought and/or that you yourself may be contributing to the performance problem or the difficult response.

Table 4.1 Dealing with difficult responses to negative feedback

Difficult response	Don't ...	Do ...
Anger/attack: The person becomes angry and lashes out at you.	Counter-attack, become defensive, or get involved in a shouting match.	Acknowledge the anger and solicit the person's feedback. Also, you may need to clarify that the review process is about behaviours and results, not about the person's character. *Example*: 'It sounds like you're angry about this process. Can you tell me more about why you are angry?' or 'It sounds like you're angry about this process. I just want to emphasise that this feedback is not about you as a person, but about specific behaviours that have occurred.'
Defensiveness/ denial: The person denies the accuracy of your observations and feedback, or tries to deny its importance.	Ignore the person's viewpoint or, on the other hand, get involved in a tit-for-tat conversation.	Accept the possibility they know something you don't and solicit specific observable evidence. Be ready to (re)state the evidence on which you based your feed-back. *Example:* 'It seems like we have a different perspective here. Can you pinpoint what in my assessment you find inaccu-rate or unfair?'

Table 4.1 cont.

Passing the buck: The person blames poor performance on the lack of tools, assistance, resources, time or other support.	Ignore the complaints or, on the other hand, let the person avoid responsibility for their performance.	Acknowledge the concerns and encourage the person to focus on what he or she can control. *Example*: 'It sounds like you have some frustrations. Why don't you list them for me, and when we're done with the review we'll come back and address those issues. In the meantime, why don't we focus on what is under your control.'
Silence: The person is uninvolved in the conversation and says little or nothing.	Keep talking as if nothing is wrong.	Acknowledge the silence, express your concern and ask for their thoughts. *Example*: 'I notice you're not saying much, I'm concerned that there is some-thing on your mind. What can you tell me about it?'
Indifference: The person hears and understands the issues but doesn't seem to care.	Ignore the indifference or chastise the person for lack of commitment.	Point out the apparent indifference, and then make clear how the issue affects them, you and the team. *Example*: 'I'm getting a sense that this issue doesn't matter much to you. But before you reach that conclusion, let's talk about how it impacts on you and the team.'
Despair: The person takes the feedback very hard and feels inadequate and/or discouraged.	Ignore the person's feelings or, on the other hand, tell them to 'buck up'.	Acknowledge their frustration or sadness and give them space to talk about it. Remind them that the feedback is about specific performance issues, not their value as a person. Look for opportunities to create small successes. *Example*: 'It must be hard for you to hear this. I value your contribution, and this feed-back is not meant to reflect on you as a person.'

A six-step process for giving negative feedback effectively

1. Find out what the person was trying to achieve.

2. Tell the person exactly what you have observed.

3. Explain how you feel about the employee's actions and the impact of his or her behaviour on what they were trying to achieve.

4. Solicit feedback.

5. Show support and coach for possible solutions.

6. Get a commitment to improve behaviour.

As noted by Sir John Whitmore:

> Feedback from ourselves and from others is vital for learning and performance improvement. That feedback needs to cover both the results of the action and the action process itself.
>
> The important thing, if we truly wish to bring the best out of people, is to fundamentally rethink and refocus. Our primary objective must be to understand what the client needs in order to perform the task well, and to ask, say or do whatever it takes to help them to meet that need. Our own wish to be in control, or to display our superior knowledge, or simply our laziness to give up old habits and change, will need to be set aside if we want them to perform. It is hard to break the prevailing mould of behaviour, but break it we must.

The power of constructive feedback

Constructive feedback increases self-awareness, offers options and can motivate. It does not only mean giving positive feedback – feedback about poor performance, given skilfully, can be equally useful and important as an aid to development.

Working with feedback

Feedback needs to be *useful*, that is to say someone needs to make use of it. Can they do that if they take issue with it or if it upsets them so much that they miss the point? The following guidelines can help you, as a coach, work with feedback effectively.

1. *Give with care.* To be useful, feedback requires the giver to feel concern for and to care for the person receiving the feedback – to want to help, not to hurt the other person.

2. *Give with attention.* It is important to pay attention to what you are doing as you give feedback. This helps you engage in a two-way exchange with some depth of communication.

3. *Invited by the recipient.* Feedback is most effective when the receiver has invited comments. This provides a platform for openness and some guidelines and it also gives the receiver an opportunity to identify and explore particular areas of concern.

4. *Directly expressed.* Good feedback is specific and deals clearly with particular incidents and behaviour.

Making vague statements and generalisations is of little value. The most useful feedback is direct, open and concrete.

5. *Fully expressed*. Effective feedback requires more than a bald statement of facts. Feelings also need to be expressed so that the receiver can judge the full impact of their behaviour.

6. *Uncluttered by evaluative judgements*. Often it is helpful not to give feedback composed of judgements or evaluations. If you wish to offer judgements then it is necessary to state clearly that these matters are of subjective evaluation and then to simply describe the situation as you see it and let the person concerned make the evaluation.

7. *Well timed*. The most useful feedback is given when the receiver is receptive to it and it is sufficiently close to the particular event being discussed for it to be fresh in their mind. Storing comments can lead to a build-up of recriminations and reduces the effectiveness of feedback when it is finally given.

8. *Readily actionable*. Feedback that centres around behaviour that can be changed by the receiver is more useful than feedback that concerns matters outside their control. It is often helpful to suggest alternative ways of behaving that allow the receiver to think about new ways of tackling old problems.

9. *Agree what feedback is being called for first*. This can help the feedback session stay focused and fits in with the performance management process.

10. *Balanced*. It is worthwhile putting a structure to the feedback session to ensure there is a balance between positive and negative behaviours in the context of what they are trying to achieve. Working with *negative* first, then *interesting* and finishing with *positive* feedback is one way of doing this.

Potential barriers to effective feedback

Parsloe and Wray (2000) have identified several barriers to both giving and receiving feedback:

- Feedback can come as a surprise or shock when there are no clear objectives for the job or development, or when the learner and the coach or mentor do not share the same perception of these.
- The feedback may be delivered in a way that the recipient sees as concentrating on critical or unsubstantiated judgements which offend against the recipient's sense of fairness.
- There may be a problem of credibility. It is important that the recipient believes that the feedback-giver is competent to comment on those points.
- Their previous history of receiving negative feedback may make the recipient feel obliged to 'defend their corner'.
- People are afraid to give feedback because they are not confident about handling the response and are concerned that feedback will damage relationships.

The following two models look at giving feedback. Called ORCE and NIP they are useful for developing the giving of feedback from an observational stance.

The NIP model for feedback

The PIN model was designed and utilised very effectively in the Eastern Bloc countries prior to the fall of the Berlin Wall. Its primary use was in sports coaching and it relied on the adrenaline within the body to overcome the abruptness of the approach.

In business we reverse the process from that used in sport and it becomes NIP (see Figure 4.6). In sports coaching the results are more immediate and have the benefit of adrenaline – in business we do not have this luxury.

The coach is directive in their approach and should work through the model. The first stage, as with all feedback, is

---

Ask: What were you trying to achieve?

N – Negative

The coach states objectively what was negative about the performance in light of what they were trying to achieve.

I – Interesting

The coach then asks for comments on an interesting observation of the performance by the client.

P – Positive

The coach states what was positive about the performance after observing.

Figure 4.6 The NIP model for feedback.

to *ascertain what the client was trying to achieve in the first place*. By finding this out any feedback will be within the client's frame of reference.

With the NIP model use only *one* negative point, *one* interesting point and *one* positive point. This way the model is much more balanced. Logically, if you think about it, if someone was to give you more than one negative point you probably wouldn't hear the second as you would be rerunning the conversation and justifying things in your own mind.

By asking the client what they found interesting, they are moving themselves away from the negativity of the first point, instead of you trying to talk them away from it.

The question is, 'If you can only give one point, which would it be?' It has to be the one that will have the most impact on what they are trying to achieve.

The final point is to develop and build on what is positive. Giving a genuine positive point at the end of the session will build confidence and encourage the client to develop. It is the feedback equivalent of the 'one good shot in a game of golf that always makes you want to come back'.

The coach has to agree that this model is acceptable to the client, which is usually established during the contract. The coach then has to establish its suitability for the client and the situation before using it.

Introduction to ORCE

ORCE is an analysis tool that is beneficial not only for coaching but also for gathering data for giving feedback.

One of the essential skills of any coach is to be able to observe what is happening and to recognise specific behaviours which are helping or hindering an individual's performance. We may define behaviours generally here as:

- What a person says.
- What a person does.

Generally speaking people feel comfortable about discussing behaviours as long as the focus is on the facts.

Between actions being performed and feedback being given there are four stages according to the ORCE analysis tool. These four stages are outlined in Figure 4.7.

The memory is a fragile beast, especially if the feedback is about something that did not go too well. The ORCE analysis tool can be used in coaching or in general management.

O – Observation – watching what is actually happening.

R – Recording – taking notes of actual behaviours (what is said and done).

C – Classifying – classifying the behaviours that were visible, e.g. tone, volume, posture.

E – Evaluating – deciding if the observations are positive or negative evidence of the desired behaviours.

Figure 4.7 The ORCE analysis tool.

Working with metaphors and clean language

While I have been using metaphors for many years I was introduced to the concept of 'clean language' a while back by Sue Knight who had asked James Lawley and Penny Tomkins to facilitate a day on an NLP (Neuro Linguistic Programming) Master Practioner Programme that Sue was running. The result was sublime to say the least. To say that James and Penny were masters of the art is a gross understatement. They have taken the concept of metaphors to bits like mechanics and rebuilt it like artists.

The concept of clean language was initially introduced by David Grove, a New Zealander whose unique psycho-therapeutic approach, experience and style makes him one of today's most skilful and innovative therapists. In the 1980s he developed clinical methods for resolving clients' dramatic memories, especially those related to child abuse, rape and incest. He realised many clients naturally described their symptoms using metaphors and found that when he enquired about these using the clients' exact words, their perception of trauma began to change. This led him to create clean language, a way of asking questions of clients' metaphors which neither contaminate nor distort them.

To figure out what David Grove was doing during this process James Lawley and Penny Tompkins used the process called modelling. This involved many observations of him working with clients. During this time they looked for patterns in the relationship between what he was doing and the way the clients responded that contributed to the changes they experienced. They combined these patterns into a generalised model, which was tested and fine-tuned – cycling through observation, pattern detection and model destruction, construction, testing and revising many times. James and Penny also drew upon cognitive linguistics, self-organising systems theory and NLP and the result is a process called symbolic modelling.

Symbolic modelling is a method for facilitating individuals to become familiar with the symbolic domain of their experience so that they can discover new ways of perceiving themselves and their world. It uses clean language to help them to listen to their metaphoric expressions so that they create a model of their symbolic mind/body perceptions. This model exists as a living, breathing, four-dimensional world within and around them. When clients explore this world and its inherent logic their metaphors and way of being are honoured. During the therapeutic process their metaphors begin to evolve, and as this happens their everyday thinking, feeling and behaviour correspondingly change as well. Some clients benefit from just having their metaphors developed with a few clean questions, for some the process leads to a reorganisation of their existing symbolic perceptions, while for others nothing short of a transformation of their entire landscape of metaphors will suffice. As a result clients report that they are more self-aware, more at peace with themselves, have a more defined sense of their place in the world and are more able to enrich the lives of others.

The symbolic domain of experience

There are three domains of experience referred to as the sensory, conceptual and symbolic:

1. *Sensory.* People know about the environment, the material world and the behaviour of themselves and others through seeing, hearing, touching, smelling and tasting, and by their emotions and inner-body feelings of orientation, movement, balance and position. People also see pictures, hear sounds, feel feelings in their imagination when they remember a past event or imagine a future happening.

2. *Conceptual.* All categories, comparisons, beliefs and judgements are constructs of the human mind – they only exist as abstract concepts. While everyone has experienced being part of a group of related people no one has ever touched the concept 'family'. Concepts are a different order of reality from the sensory material world. Concepts are labels to complex gestalts of experience.

3. *Symbolic.* A number of philosophers, linguists and cognitive scientists claim that much, if not most, of everyday language and thinking is neither sensory nor conceptual but is actually metaphoric. Metaphors allow people to express and give form to complex feelings, behaviours, situations and abstract concepts. Most metaphors make use of the sensory material world to describe, comprehend and reason about the conceptual and abstract. For James Lawley and Penny Tompkins 'symbolic' means more than the dictionary

definition of 'relating to a symbol', it also involves connecting with a pattern that has personal significance.

In their book *Metaphors in Mind* (2000) Penny and James refer to the distinctions between the domains which they related to the American flag with sensory, perceptual and symbolic language. In my case I could talk about my first car.

Describing something in *sensory* terms requires a specific example and words that directly relate to what we see, hear or feel. In this case it was made of steel and was Savannah beige in colour. It had twin 'Hella' spot lamps on the front that would illuminate when the headlights were put on main beam. It had an 'Ansa' racing exhaust that increased the acceleration and noise. It had low-profile tyres which improved the road holding. (It's only when writing about this in later years that you realise how daft this must have appeared to on-lookers!)

The *conceptual* label was a '1300 Volkswagen Beetle'.

The *symbolic* description of 'Alexander' (taken from the A.A. Milne poem) varied from person to person. To me it was 'My first car' symbolising 'Freedom'. To my dad, it was a 'good car that I had spoiled'. To my brother it symbolised 'the freedom to have a drink' when we drove from Newport Pagnell to Villa Park in Birmingham, when it was my turn to drive! To my Mum it was Herbie (after the Walt Disney film)! If we were to pursue the matter further, people who were involved with 'Alexander' would have different recollections of what this car meant to them – especially the local constabulary, who stopped me on more than one occasion to check the sound levels of the exhaust!

So there you have the three types of description – sensory, conceptual and symbolic. They represent distinct, yet interrelated, ways of perceiving the world.

The development of the metaphor

George Lakoff and Mark Johnson have defined a metaphor as follows: 'The essence of a metaphor is the understanding and experiencing of one kind of thing in the terms of another'. The symbol, however, is slightly more elusive. Carl Jung noted that there is something more to the symbol than meets the eye, no matter how much it is described. Penny and James refer to a symbol as a term, a name or even a picture that maybe familiar in daily life, yet possesses specific connotations in addition to its conventional and obvious meaning. It implies something vague, unknown or hidden from us. Metaphors have a unique quality. The form of a metaphor is different from the original experience, but it has similar organisation. This is often referred to as isomorphism. This means that the attributes of the symbol in the relationships between the symbols and the logic of the whole match the organisation of what is being described. For example, the expression of passion in sport is often referred to as 'fire in the belly' of the competitor. This is the unique quality of what we are referring to, i.e. 'fire' and 'burn'. The key role of the metaphor is to capture the essence, the intangible, between the lines, relationships and patterns. Isomorphism is the pattern which connects two different kinds of things. When a person comprehends a metaphor it is their intrinsic ability to recognise and utilise isomorphism that allows them to infer the organisation of the original experience from the metaphor. This can be achieved by empathic divining (see p. 51).

Metaphors can be classified into four groups: verbal, non-verbal, material and imaginative.

Verbal metaphors

With the verbal metaphor we refer to the words and phrases that are obviously and conventionally metamorphic as overt verbal metaphors. This distinguishes them from the less obvious verbal metaphors embedded in everyday speech. There is nothing absolute about this distinction – it depends entirely upon the listener or the speaker's awareness of the metaphors used in the language. Although embedded metaphors are not usually recognised as metaphorical, they are an essential and universal feature of language. Examples of overt verbal metaphors include:

- I've got my head in the clouds.
- I'm carrying the whole world on my shoulders.
- I've got a knot in my stomach.

An embedded verbal metaphor is slightly different. When everyday language is examined in detail the power of the metaphor is far more common than first realised – in fact it is 'hard' to 'put together' an 'everyday' sentence which does not 'contain' a 'hidden' or 'embedded' metaphor. Typical examples are:

- My mind has just gone blank.
- There is a gap in my knowledge.
- I'm feeling down today.
- I'm going round in circles.

Non-verbal metaphors

Non-verbal metaphors are slightly different from the norm. Although metaphors are generally thought of as linguistic devices, non-verbal behaviour, bodily expressions and non-verbal sounds can also be metaphoric. They are metaphoric in that they can be used to understand an experience of one kind of thing in terms of another. When clients pay attention to their bodily expressions, a symbolic world just outside of awareness is revealed. For example, one client discovered that a grabbing movement with their hands out in front symbolised holding on when they really needed to let go. Another client with a hunched posture found that this expressed a feeling of having the whole world on their shoulders, while a client who sat motionless, leaning forward and staring down was surprised to find the angle of their gaze represented looking over the edge into a bottomless pit. Non-verbal sounds such as throat clears, sighs, clicks, blows, giggles and aha, oh, hum, hmmm or humming noises may regularly be encoded with symbolic meaning. For example, a client who regularly cleared their throat before speaking found that it symbolised 'being unable to speak my truth'. Another's nervous giggle, whenever they were complimented, 'prevented their pride that comes before a fall'.

Material metaphors

The mind has a remarkable capacity for seeing, hearing and feeling symbolism in the material object or the environment. Penny and James noted in their consulting room that shadows, wallpaper, carpet patterns, curtains, ornaments, pictures, book titles, mirrors, furniture, door handles, etc. have caught a client's attention and activated a symbolic response. They have lost count of the number of times the client has remarked on the shape, size, colour and layout of something in the consulting room, or their clothes or jewellery coincidentally matches a symbol in their imagination. Given the choice, clients attempt to position themselves so there is a maximum alignment between the configuration of their inner symbolic world and the layout of the physical environment. This may mean sitting where they can see out the window, being near a door, or having us on their left or their right. Therapists usually follow a particular practice asking clients to choose where they would like to sit and then position themselves. Their preferences invariably turn out to have some degree of symbolic significance. I have found myself looking at a client's bookshelves in the past only to make a connection with something they say later that has some significance.

Imaginative metaphors

In addition to material, non-verbal and verbal symbolic expression there is another imaginative metaphor which occurs in the private world of thoughts and feelings, the seeing of objects and events in the mind's eye, the hearing of sounds and internal dialogue with the feeling of emotions and other sensations which together create a personalised version of reality. To have a conscious, imaginative representation requires the imagined object of perception to be located somewhere in the mind's space. This is a further development of traditional visualisation.

Visualisation works because of the ability of clients to notice what is in their imaginative mind space to which they then have very real responses. Changes to imaginative representations have been correlated with changes in heart rate, galvanic skin response, blood pressure and a list of other chemical and neurophysiological effects.

During symbolic modelling Penny and James regard the client's imaginative realm as existing in a perceptual space that is as real as any physical environment. This space can exist inside and outside their body, or in an entirely imaginative environment happening somewhere and 'somewhen' else. Exactly as described, recognising and honouring their experience can help clients discover the metaphors they live by.

Metaphoric translation

Because the four categories of symbolic expression are interrelated it is possible to translate a metaphor from one form to another. In symbolic modelling there are two common forms of translation: verbalising and physicalising. Much of the symbolic modelling process involves facilitating the client to verbalise the symbolism they ascribe to their imaginative representations, their non-verbal behaviour and the material objects that draw their attention. The other type of translation involves the client physicalising their spoken and imaginative metaphors, that is intentionally creating a physical, symbolic representation, which may be through drawing, painting, sculpting, poetry, prose or music, or they could use their body to mime, act or dance their metaphor. Physically a metaphor often enables clients to depict things that they cannot say to encapsulate and convey the wholeness of an experience in a single, material representation.

There is a five-stage therapeutic process that is a framework for facilitating clients to self-model the way their metaphorical landscape is organised and evolved (see Figure 4.8).

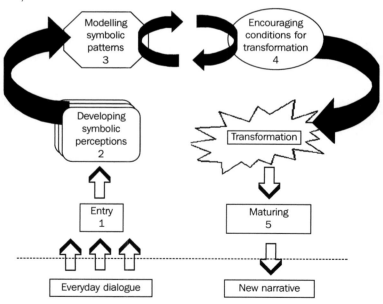

Reproduced by kind permission of James Lawley and Penny Tomkins from their publication *Metaphors in Mind*. ISBN 0 9538751 0 5. *www.cleanlanguage.co.uk*

Figure 4.8 The five-stage therapeutic process.

Stage 1: Entry

The horizontal dashed line in Figure 4.8 denotes a threshold between two worlds: below the line is everyday narrative, conceptual description of dialogue and above the line is the embodied metaphor, symbolic perceptions and trialogue. During Stage 1 clients become aware that their verbal and non-verbal expressions as well as objects and events in the physical environment can be perceived metaphorically. This requires only the merest shift of attention from commonplace recounting of events to engaging with the world of personal symbolism. Entry into this symbolic domain can happen spontaneously, or it can be facilitated by a clean question.

Stage 2: Developing symbolic perceptions

Stage 2 focuses on developing a single symbolic perception. A symbolic perception encompasses a unit of symbolic time that need have little obvious relation to a clock or remembered time. It can be a moment, an event, a scene, a process or even an entire lifetime. It allows an instant to be examined for hours, or an eon to be explored in a few minutes. During Stage 2 clients individuate the components of each symbolic perception from the undifferentiated information mass they typically bring to therapy. When the matrix of their experience differentiates into symbols which have existence and an identity, each symbol's attributes and their relationship with other symbols become apparent. As clients give form to and engage with their symbol a symbolic perception forms and comes to life, like a photograph emerging from a developing solution. The client can then be asked to draw or in some other way physicalise the configuration of the symbols and relationships.

Stage 3: Modelling symbolic patterns

Clients make the transition to Stage 3 when multiple perceptions have been developed and a more complex metaphoric landscape emerges. The landscape creates a context in which the patterns across perception can be identified and examined. Patterns manifest as stable configurations, repeating sequences and recurring motives (over space, across time and among attributes). Once identified each pattern can be named, symbolically represented and explored, thus the modelling process repeats at a higher and more inclusive level. As the organising of logic and the metaphoric landscape is revealed the client discovers:

- the role of the configuration of symbols and relationships;
- the sequence in which thoughts, feelings and behaviours repeat time and time again;
- the significance of recurring motifs in the overall scheme;
- resources which can beneficially influence the landscape;
- binding patterns whose organisation prevents change and maintains the status quo;
- how the system can evolve – when as a result of self-knowledge change occurs spontaneously, Stage 4 is bypassed and the change is matured in Stage 5.

Stage 4: Encouraging conditions for transformation

If change does not occur spontaneously, or if the change translates the 'present state' into another form without changing its essential nature (the classic 'jumping out of the frying pan into the fire'), a binding pattern of patterns, a double bind, will be maintaining the metaphoric landscape's existing organisation. In these cases a transformation to a new form of organisation is required.

Stage 5: Maturing

When the form, location or function of a symbol changes, the effects of that change can be matured in Stage 5. Maturing is a process by which a newly changed symbol is evolved, developed and differentiated from its previous form, and the effects of the change spread to other symbols. When sufficient changes accumulate or a change of sufficient significance occurs, thresholds are exceeded, boundaries are crossed, defining moments occur and binding patterns transform. Then a new organisation emerges which transcends and includes the limitations of the existing landscape. After further maturing, the new landscape takes on solidity and a life of its own. Now the client can contemplate the changes that have taken place, become familiar with their new symbolic world and make new associations. As this happens cognition, perception and behaviour change accordingly.

Team coaching

There has been much said about team coaching in the past, but there is very little evidence written up in such a way that actually makes it useful to anybody trying to develop their team coaching skills. In this section I hope to set out some of the key requirements for team coaching that we have found useful in the past and that can help you build and develop your own team coaching skills.

Probably one of the single biggest pieces of research, in terms of teams and how they work, was created by Jon Katzenbach and Douglas Smith. In their book *The Wisdom of Teams* (2003) they outline some common-sense findings which basically people know but do not apply to teams in any disciplined way. If there is one thing that the coach can actually do it's bring a degree of focus and discipline to the whole aspect of team performance and enhancement. One of the key components for a coach in the field of team coaching is the ability to see the big picture yet have a keen eye for detail, and these are often seen as conflicting qualities. However, many sports team coaches have these abilities and deploy them correctly.

Let us start with the common-sense findings, of which the first is that a demanding performance challenge has a tendency to create a team. The desire for performance is actually one of the greatest attributes of team success, more so than any other traditional approach to team building – this includes charismatic team leaders and is above and beyond incentives and team-building away-days. The second common-sense finding that was developed in their book was that the disciplined application of 'team basics' was very often overlooked. The team basics are outlined in Figure 4.9. Katzenbach and Smith (2003) maintained that if any of these areas were missing in terms of the team basics the possibility that the team would be derailed was very high.

The third common-sense finding is that team performance opportunities are apparent and exist in all parts of the organisation. This is one more opportunity for the coach to look for as many teams within organisations are obvious, such as project teams, re-engineering teams, sales teams, etc.

Figure 4.9 Focusing on team basics.

However, there is an opportunity to develop teamwork and effective teams in all parts of the organisation and once again Katzenbach and Smith (2003) maintain that there is a lot of team performance that is actually untapped potential within the world of work.

The fourth of the common-sense findings was that the teams at the top were the most difficult. Any coach or facilitator that has actually worked with a team of non-executives or the board can fully appreciate this. This is a complex area to work in as they are dealing with long-term challenges in terms of strategy. In addition, their time is very limited and there is a degree of ingrained individualism which Katzenbach and Smith believe conspires against teams at the top. Indeed, in many cases you will see fewer teams at the top of large organisations and where you do see teams there are fewer people in them.

Most organisations intrinsically prefer the individual over the group (team accountability). I have seen this in many instances – we have schemes such as performance-related pay based on individual performance, and we have one-to-ones with individuals as opposed to team coaching sessions. (This latter is not just in name only – there are very few team coaching sessions that actually occur at work. Where you do see them they will be in one of the team basic areas, as outlined in Figure 4.9.) So taking on board these two aspects – the common-sense findings of Katzenbach and Smith plus the team basics – coaches certainly have their work cut out.

While in the main we have advocated the approach of non-directive coaching, there is a case here to be directive with the process but non-directive with the team. For example, it is important that the coach ensures that any of the team basics that are missing are identified by the team and rectified by the team, not by the coach. We have found that a small audit is useful to identify which one of the three areas – skills, accountability and commitment – are lacking in the team basics triangle. This area can then be broken down even further to look at, for example in the skills area, where the problem-solving skills lie, where the technical/functional skills lie and where the interpersonal skills lie (though all members of the team should have a degree of these). Just as Belbin identifies primary and secondary team types in his characteristic team type inventory, I would advocate that team players here should have a primary basic function and a secondary basic function. But I would also advocate that they need a third basic function – that is to provide support for each other. This means you are looking for a certain amount of coaching qualities within each of the individuals within the team. The small audit, from the coach's point of view, could take on the format of Figure 4.10.

Key deficiencies	How to overcome
To be identified by the team and the coach	To be coached out of the team (i.e. the team knows them and this information needs to be gleaned from the team).

Figure 4.10 Format of the small team audit.

Now we have considered the common-sense approach and some of the team basics, the other thing we need to be aware of as a coach is what is referred to as the team performance curve. The team performance curve has been labelled many things and more recently its main aspects have been referred to as forming, storming, norming and performing. While in this book we do not wish to go into these aspects of team building, from a coach's point of view it is useful to identify at which stage the team is located. So, as illustrated in Figure 4.11, what we have are five stages.

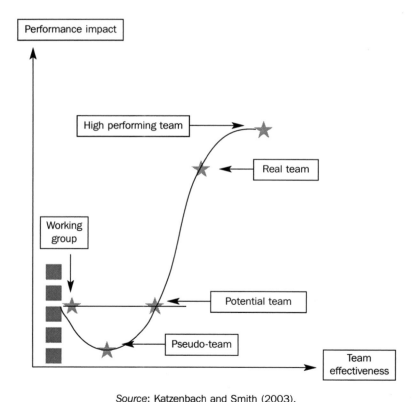

Source: Katzenbach and Smith (2003).

Figure 4.11 The team performance curve.

1. *The working group.* This is identified by Katzenbach and Smith (2003) as the group of people for which there is no 'significant incremental performance, need, or opportunity that would require it to become a team'. This is the kind of working group that we see in many places in many organisations and is the one that we were referring to earlier when we said that opportunities exist all over the organisation.

2. *The pseudo-team.* Following Katzenbach and Smith's definition, this is the group for which there could be 'a significant incremental performance need or opportunity'. However, there is a lack of focus here, both individually and collectively, and therefore people are unaware of it. One of the key principles of coaching is to raise awareness, and it is the same for teams as it is for individuals.

3. *The potential team.* This is the group for which there is a 'significant incremental performance need and [which] is really trying to improve its performance impact'. In this case it usually is a lack of clarity around the team basics and around the common purpose, to be discussed later. There are many aspects of the team basics triangle that are actually missing, in particular the collective accountability.

4. *The real team.* This refers to a small number of people 'with complementary skills who are equally committed to a common purpose, goals and a working approach for which they hold themselves mutually accountable'. This is probably the team that most organisations

would want to have and many blindly believe that they do have. However, this is the one area where the coach can really come into play. The coach can have an input in other areas, obviously in terms of the working group, the pseudo-team and the potential team, and certainly in the field of potential teams there is a lot of scope and room for manoeuvre. However, the real team is about maintaining the status quo of current performance while allowing the team themselves to identify where continuous improvement could be achieved. This takes us on to the next level, the high performance team.

5. *High performance teams*. This group usually meets all of the terms and conditions of the team's charter and requirements, but there is also a learning edge to this team as well. In terms of the commitment aspect of team basics, not only do they meet the specified goals, the common approach and the meaningful purpose, there is also a personal growth aspect and a mutual accountability for each other's personal growth as well. This is where people really 'go into bat' for each other and the coach is used to help and facilitate with that growth.

The team leader

The team leader has a key role to play in any team, especially when it comes to developing a potential team or maturing into a real team or even a high performance one, but there can be a tendency for the coach to coach the team leader and let the team leader then coach the team which somewhat muddies the waters. There is an opportunity here to coach both the team and the team leader. Given what we have discussed regarding confidentiality and how the coach keeps a balanced approach to the role, what the coach can do is act as both the individual and team coach by keeping the activities and conversations as separate entities. Thus the team leader can learn from the coach, by observing and working with the coach's approach to the team.

Many people believe that it is the selection of the team leader that is the crucial aspect. While we do not discount this it should be noted that that a lot of work can be done by the coach once the team leader is in place. It is my belief that teams can actually move through the team performance curve a lot quicker if a coach is appointed at the same time as the team leader and facilitates both the learning curve of the team leader and the team performance during the first three months of the team's initiation or induction.

There are some key questions to be asked of the team leader by the coach during and after this three-month period. One of the key areas we are looking for is to see the approach that the leader has adopted, especially comparing a team approach and a working group approach as this can give us some early pointers as to how the team will actually navigate the performance curve. For example, does the leader make all the important decisions and allocate all the work assignments? Do they make all evaluations of the individuals, or are there evaluations of the team or sub-teams? Does the leader ensure work is conducted on the basis of individual accountability or joint accountability? Does the leader do any actual work, over and above decision-making, delegating and agenda-setting? These questions, when asked at this stage, are a good litmus test of how the team leader is performing.

On the softer side there are some further questions you can ask here, in particular whether the team leader is striving for the right balance between action and patience within the team. For example, does the leader balance the constructive conflicts and resolution within the team? Do they use distance and perspective, i.e. the big picture and focusing on specifics, to keep the team's actions and directions relevant? Do they challenge the team to sharpen their purpose and goals and approach, or do they just leave these be once they have been set? Are they inspiring in terms of trust by acting in accordance with the team's purpose and do they create opportunities for others, sometimes at their own or other's expense? The answers to these questions can certainly point the way towards the emotional intelligence quota of the leader which is an important factor.

Still keeping in the soft vein but taking a more subtle approach, some of the things we need to look at are how the leader actually communicates – the true leader will subliminally, as well as consciously, articulate the team purpose and promote and share responsibility for it. For example, does the leader think about and describe the assignments in individual or team terms? The answer to this question will let you know where the leader is coming from. Do they identify and act to remove barriers to team performance or are they continually vocalising individual aspects? Do they ever blame individuals for failure to perform, whether it be of the team or not? Do they ever excuse the shortfalls in performance by pointing to outside factors? As a coach, by just listening to the types of conversations the leader has one can determine where the leader's mindset is – you are looking for it to be predominantly team rather than individually based.

The checklist given in Table 4.2 provides a useful audit for the coach, the leader or the team members of the group's current situation. It is based around the six basic elements of a team as defined by Katzenbach and Smith (2003).

Table 4.2 Audit checklist of current situation

Size (small enough in number)	Yes ✓	No ✗
1. Can you convene easily and frequently?		
2. Can you communicate with all members easily and frequently?		
3. Are your discussions open and interactive for all members?		
4. Does each member understand the others' roles and skills?		
5. Do you need more people to achieve your ends?		
6. Are sub-teams possible or necessary?		
Skills (adequate levels)	✓	✗
1. Are all three categories of skills either actually or potentially represented across the membership (functional/technical, problem-solving/decision-making and interpersonal)?		
2. Does each member have the potential in all three categories to advance his or her skills to the level required by the team's purpose and goals?		

Table 4.2 cont.

	Yes	No
3. Are any skill areas that are critical to team performance missing or under-represented?		
4. Are the members, individually and collectively, willing to spend more time to help themselves and others learn and develop skills?		
5. Can you introduce new or supplemental skills as needed?		
Purpose (truly meaningful purpose)	✓	✗
1. Does it constitute a broader, deeper aspiration than just near-term goals?		
2. Is it a team purpose as opposed to a broader organisational purpose or just one individual's purpose (e.g. the leader's)?		
3. Do all members understand and articulate it the same way? And do they do so without relying on ambiguous abstractions?		
4. Do members define it vigorously in discussions with outsiders?		
5. Do members frequently refer to it and explore its implications?		
6. Does it contain themes that are particularly meaningful and memorable?		
7. Do members feel it is important, if not exciting?		
Goals (specific goal or goals)	✓	✗
1. Are they team goals versus broader organisational goals or just one individual's goals (e.g. the leader's)?		
2. Are they clear, simple and measurable? If not measurable, can their achievement be determined?		
3. Are they realistic as well as ambitious? Do they allow small wins along the way?		

Table 4.2 cont.

	Yes	No
4. Do they call for a concrete set of team work-products?		
5. Is their relative importance and priority clear to all members?		
6. Do all members agree with the goals, their relative importance and the way in which their achievement will be measured?		
7. Do all members articulate the goals in the same way?		
Approach (clear working approach)	✓	✗
1. Is the approach concrete, clear and really understood and agreed by everybody? Will it result in achievement of the objectives?		
2. Will it capitalise on and enhance the skills of all members? Is it consistent with other demands on the members?		
3. Does it require all members to contribute equivalent amounts of real work?		
4. Does it provide for open interaction, fact-based problem-solving and results-based evaluation?		
5. Do all members articulate the approach in the same way?		
6. Does it provide for modification and improvement over time?		
7. Are fresh input and perspectives systematically sought and added, for example through information and analysis, new members and senior sponsors?		
Accountability (sense of mutual accountability)	✓	✗
1. Are you individually and jointly accountable for the team's purpose, goals, approach and work-products?		

Table 4.2 cont.

	Yes	No
2. Can you and do you measure progress against specific goals? .		
3. Do all members feel responsible for all measures?		
4. Are the members clear on what they are individually responsible for and what they are jointly responsible for?		
5. Is there a sense that 'only the team can fail'?		

Ethics in coaching

For most people ethics means something esoteric, impractical and far removed from reality, but coaching ethics aren't mysterious. It is about us as coaches. People working with other people, making decisions in our own mind and getting people to make decisions in organisations every day. In most cases ethics revolve around cynicism; however, the coach has moved beyond cynicism as described in Chapter 3 in the section on developing relationships. It is about building trust and the respect to ensure that the right conditions apply. Much of the problem and controversy around ethics is based around its definition. Ethics can be defined as a set of moral principles or values and this portrays them as highly personal and relative, but for the purposes of the coach a better definition would be the principles, norms and standards of conduct governing a coach/client relationship, as well as coaching practice.

In the twenty-first century ethics is the culmination of deciding what is right and doing what is right, as opposed to the philosophical arguments that were put forward back in the eighteenth, nineteenth and early twentieth centuries. It is also worth pointing out that in today's world we live in a shroud of legal and cultural constraints, and while the litigious society in the United States is very different from the United Kingdom, many people believe the latter is catching up. So let us have a look at ethics and what this means for the coach. It predominantly falls into five key areas and the first is *contracting*.

The idea of the contract is to state your intentions as a coach and to remove any ambiguity, misunderstanding or misconceptions. The contract should set out your ethical stall for your client to purchase from. A useful question to ask is: 'Does your contract set out this stall?' Within this falls the issue of confidentiality. Confidentiality is built via the relationship and maintained through trust as mentioned in the section on developing the relationship in Chapter 3. However, there are usually three parties involved: the coach, the client and the purchasing organisation. One ethical dilemma that we had on many occasions in the latter part of the twentieth century when organisations were restructuring, re-engineering and downsizing was where executive coaching was coming up against individuals who were trying to engineer themselves out of the organisation while not telling anybody. In these particular cases it was only the use of a robust contract at the outset that prevented the coach from having many ethical problems and sleepless nights. On a more everyday practical approach, I have heard several conversations in the past start off with the words, 'Whatever we say is within these four walls' – as you would expect, it is a somewhat naive promise to make as one has no idea, as the coach, where the conversation is going to go. I remember one manager making this rash promise while interviewing a member of staff for poor performance only to find out in the middle of the conversation that the individual had their 'fingers in the till'. The manager had a dilemma: did he report the individual thus breaking his promise, or did he not report the individual thus violating his managerial contract and responsibilities? It is one that the manager wrestled with and eventually coached the individual to own up outside of the contractual arrangement that they had.

The agreement of confidentiality is built around the status of communication between the coach and the client. As mentioned earlier in the United States, such communication is not 'privileged' as in the case of the lawyer and the client. Coaching records have been subpoenaed in US courts and likewise coaches have been found liable for giving misleading or irresponsible advice. There is a call for this degree of standards in the United Kingdom and the European Coaching and Mentoring Council has been developing standards which will soon be released. In the meantime, their Code of Ethics is reproduced in Appendix 1 to assist in this area.

The second area is psychological harm, and this is where counselling and coaching are very closely related. The risk of any physical harm from the coach/client relationship is minimal, but as we are now aware in the world of work it is very often the softer skills and the emotional intelligence that actually carry the heaviest burden. In this particular case you may find some degree of psychological harm such as embarrassment, anxiety or discomfort from the coach/ client relationship. It is fair to say that these things occur more in the field of life coaching than business coaching, although the two also are interrelated. When there is major change going on in the work environment then usually some of the lighter coaching skills that are used such as work/life balance and prioritising on a personal and emotional level come into play. Moving forward in the relationship it is my experience that one can sense what is going on during the course of coaching relationships, and if you start to feel a degree of discomfort then there is a moral and ethical obligation to inform the client that is where you, the coach, are at that point in time. It may be that you are out of your depth. As such it is useful to be able to refer your client to other specialists that would be able to competently conduct these particular parts of the coaching sessions. Moving back again into the contract the coach really has to obtain informed consent from the client that it is quite acceptable for the coach to do this during the process. Indeed, I believe we should see some ethical guidelines for managing psychological aspects in the EMCC standards.

The third area is the limitation of competency, once again an area that we touched on in the section on developing the relationship in Chapter 3. Competency can be measured against the ten core competencies and their associated behaviours given in Appendix 2, but coaches also have to continue to learn and professionally develop their competencies by being trained, skilled and supervised in the use of the tools and techniques associated with coaching. The Chartered Institute of Professional Development (CIPD) is continually reviewing their continuing professional development (CPD) programmes for all of their members, a practice which should be mirrored by coaches. In many careers now CPD is mandatory, such as the medical profession and the legal profession. Competency is a standard that needs to be maintained. Therefore you should constantly strive to keep your 'badge' up to date yet have the ability to bring in specialists where need be. In many cases this will actually require the use of occupational psychologists who I have found to give due diligence and objective analysis thus making their involvement worthwhile. Pauline Willis of the Coaching and Mentoring Network maintains that occupational psychologists can be used in a very specialised role, in a generalist role or in a support role for the coach, client or organisation. The other aspect to consider is whether the coach is developing their competency through supervision, in which case the use of an occupational psychologist can be extremely beneficial.

The final aspect of the limits of competency involves looking at the distinctions between other related professions, such as therapy, counselling, etc. Each role has different underlying assumptions and these need to be clarified with the coach and the client. It is not a problem if the coach is a trained counsellor – indeed this can be extremely beneficial. However, what needs to be considered is which conversation the client contracted for – was it a coaching conversation or a counselling conversation? – as it would be unethical to move from one to the other without the client's awareness.

When the School of Coaching at the Industrial Society in association with Myles Downey was first started we had an abundance of people come forward for positions in the school. I remember at times conversations with Myles during the interviewing process, when Myles would ask the question: 'What do you do if the conversation with your client drifts into the arena of counselling?' In many cases the answer that came back from the potential coach was that this did not present a problem as they were trained counsellors anyway. In the post-interview debriefing with Myles, his main concern was that the potential coach was too wrapped up in their own abilities rather than considering the client's standpoint – a fatal flaw as far as Myles was concerned as Myles was and is one of the leading exponents of client-centred coaching.

The fourth area as far as ethics are concerned covers the rules for terminating the coaching assignment. There are usually rules of a contractual nature to govern this provided by the sponsoring organisation, for example 'six sessions carried out over a period of x number of months, any further work to be negotiated through and with the HR department'. However, there should be some reference to this in the individual contract that a coach is advised to put together with their client. It has to be said that the ideal situation is where the coach and the client can finish the coaching assignment with a degree of integrity and an open-door policy for continuing development. By and large this is the way that I have experienced it in the past. Many coaches have actually left the open-door environment and the relationship continues for many, many years. It is not the case that when the sponsoring organisation has finished paying the bills the whole relationship breaks down. There is usually a further development where the client and the coach actually form part of the larger network that is the coaching client fraternity in the world of business. So the ground rules for actually terminating the agreement should be discussed and developed right at the very outset. It is not about the coach saying this is how it is going to work, given that the focus is on the client here, it is how the client actually wants it to work and that discussion needs to be undertaken. But if we bear in mind the ethos of mutual trust, mutual respect and freedom of speech, it is better to have this conversation when there is no further baggage around, which is why we advocate sorting it out at the beginning.

As a way of self-assessing whether or not as a coach we are walking the talk use the following eight questions as a checklist.

1. Do I talk about the ethical implications of decisions that clients are considering?

2. Have I made it clear to the client that I do not want to be protected from bad news and do they understand that they can tell me anything without fear of retribution?

3. Do my clients talk to me and come to me with ethical dilemmas?

4. Do I provide guidance on, advice on and challenges to my client's ethical decision-making?

5. Do I consider ethical goals and well as performance and quality goals for my clients?

6. Do I focus on the means as well as the ends in my coaching process?

7. Do I require my clients to take responsibility for their decisions?

8. If I were to die tomorrow would the people I have coached say that I had integrity? How would they describe me and what would my colleagues say?

The answers to these questions should form a sound beginning for understanding your own ethical approach as a coach.

The fifth and final area concerns relationships with clients. The usual rules regarding the sexual, personal and financial exploitation of clients also apply to coaching and in the contract the boundaries have to be determined with regard to the coach's relationship with the client and their organisation. For my own part, if I am actually working with a client within an organisation on a coaching contract then it is kept totally separate from any other work that we are doing with the commissioning company. The coaching relationship is purely built around coaching – we may do other work with other departments in other areas within the same company, but the coaching relationship is usually kept separate and confidential.

Many of our programmes develop the manager as a coach and that is one of the relationships that people struggle with. An employee can understand the relationship between manager and member of staff – a manager manages people and the member of staff does the job (operational activity). What confuses the issue is that the manager does not realise that it is their job to manage people – they think that the member of staff is there to help them, the manager, to do the job (operational activity)! When the manager actually starts to coach, by asking questions and raising the employee's awareness about the job, it usually comes across 'twisted' – the manager is now trying to tell the employee how they should do the job – or, to be more accurate, how they (the manager) would do the job if they had to. The reason this falls into the area of ethics is that the manager is surreptitiously trying to get the employee to do what they want them to do without being open and honest about it, and in my opinion that is unethical.

It is interesting to note that in many organisations ethical management training is non-existent. This may throw some light on the reasons behind such scandals as Polly Peck, the Daily Mirror pension fund, Shell Petroleum, Enron and the general misrepresentation of information. Indeed, the book *New Rulers of the World* (Pilger, 2003) gives some very interesting insights into government, corporate and individual ethical relationships through the eyes of an investigative journalist.

Ethics are all about relationships. How are they built? What degree of openness exists between respective parties? Whether the relationship be between large multinationals and stakeholders like those mentioned above, between managers and employees or between coaches and clients that relationship has to be built upon trust, and constantly maintained and developed.

There needs to be a constant vigilance on the part of the coach to determine whether or not the relationships both with the organisation and with the individual are working. In conclusion there are many important concepts around ethics that need to be applied to the coaching arena in terms of your management of ethical and unethical conduct. Keep in mind that the coach is often used by individuals and organisations as a kind of inspection mirror that can be held up to reflect back the client's position from a different viewpoint. As such, most inspection mirrors work best when they are maintained and kept clean.

Switching perspectives

The ability to switch perspective and have your client do the same in a coaching relationship can very often be crucial to many major breakthroughs. The client can be locked into a particular situation through their own mindset and as such cannot see the wood for the trees. It is important then to have the tools and techniques available to facilitate the switching of the client's perspective. While there are many models that can allow this, such as the STOP tool mentioned earlier, there are other things that we as the coach can actually facilitate that are conditional and will allow the change of perspective to occur.

The first one to consider is the environment. To quote Tony Buzan once again: 'Nobody ever had an earth shattering idea sitting at their desk.' Accordingly, one of the key things we advise is to change the environment that the coaching actually occurs in. The subliminal constraints that buildings, offices, cubicles and workstations have on people are very often overlooked and it can make the coach's job a lot easier if you actually remove these elements. Moreover, if you can, remove the client to a place in which they have an interest or which creates the right conditions for forward thinking. This can not only allow the switching of perspectives but can also facilitate the breakthrough.

The second area to consider is visualisation. Professor Dave Collins of Edinburgh University has done a substantial amount of work with visualisation and athletes involving tracking the movement of muscles when an athlete is in motion and tracking similar movements in muscles when an athlete is standing still and just visualising the same run. A wonderful example of this can be seen in the video *Making Lions Roar* (Eriksson and Railo, 2002) where research was obtained on how the England football team was rebuilt after the defeat by Germany in the last game at Wembley. The key point in visualisation is that it is not just 'going through the motions once', it is actually running through the visualisation several times and each time the visualisation is run layers are built up. This not only facilitates the switching of perspectives but also allows people to positively reinforce the breakthroughs that have been made.

The next area to consider is to focus on what needs to be achieved and from whose viewpoint. In my early days of management working with McDonald's Restaurants, one of the things that was driven home to us was the use of travel paths. A travel path is where a manager or a shift manager would literally walk through the store from top to bottom viewing it from different people's viewpoints at certain areas. They would start outside the store and view it from the point of view of the customer. They would then walk through the lobby and view it from the point of view of the lobby assistant. They would approach the tills and once again view from the point of view of the customer. They would walk round the front counter and then view it from the point of view from the person operating the till. Pass the relevant workstations and view it from the point of view of the operatives. Into the backroom and view it once again from the point of view of the operatives. Up the stairs into the stock room, viewed from the point of view of the quality control aspects. Into the crew room, viewed from the point of view of the crew, and into the toilets, once again viewed in terms of McDonald's key standards of quality, service and cleanliness. What is interesting about this is that it allowed the manager to view things from different perspectives. In my executive coaching contracts I have found it most useful to take on board other people's perspectives by going to visit them and their offices. So if, for example, we are wrestling with a particular project and the aspect that we are wrestling with is the financial side of it we would go and talk to the finance director and while sitting in the finance director's office talking to them we would then look at it from their point of view. We are actually putting ourselves physically in their domain. The same thing can be done with marketing directors, production directors and a variety of other directors and their working locations. For me and my approach to coaching, I think this is one of the most beneficial aspects of managers and executives walking the job. However, they pay so much attention to trying to play the game of walking the job that the point is very often overlooked and therefore the benefit is missed.

The next area to consider is actually a combination of the two previous areas. Just imagine you are sitting at a table with two other chairs and you are trying to take on board another individual's point of view, so you are trying to switch your perspective. The way to work this particular exercise through is to sit in one chair and talk about the problem from your viewpoint, viewpoint A. By talking this through it vocalises the issue and lays it out on the table. Then change seats and move to seat number 2 and talk the problem through from the perspective of person B, once again laying it out on the table. Finally, move to seat 3 and talk the problem through from the viewpoint of person C, an independent observer. This allows you to see all the different viewpoints. Sue Knight, who first worked with me back in the early 1990s with this approach, uses modelling as a way of drawing out observations from person C's standpoint.

While in the written word that you have just read it sounds quite bizarre, it is amazing the effect that this actually has. By creating the right conditions you can realistically visualise and play out all of the different perspectives so they are out in front of you and you can then see them. This has been a useful tool in terms of coaching people for sales skills, negotiations and other areas such as conflict resolution. It not only helps you understand the goal and what the participants A, B and C are trying to achieve in their context but as a process it also helps you work through the many different perspectives that people have of the same situation.

The final point is to look at the key factors that affect most of us in our everyday work. If you look in the workplace and the way measurements are maintained they usually rotate around the following three areas: quality, cost and time. In fact many projects refer to this as the project triangle. The usefulness of this in terms of switching perspectives is to ask the client how this particular aspect relates to the quality of a particular project and get their viewpoint on that – that is one perspective. You can then ask how the same aspect relates to the cost point of view of the project and you will get a different perspective because there is a different theme involved. Needless to say you can do the same exercise with time and get yet another perspective. This is particularly useful considering this is how most projects are managed and therefore allows you to switch perspectives and focus on what needs to be achieved, allows visualisation and facilitates the process. The key point in switching perspectives is to try and get as much dimensionality to the issue as possible. It is similar to looking at a picture on the wall and looking at a model which you can walk around. You can look at the different elevations, the different profiles and get a lot more information by walking around a model than looking at a two-dimensional picture of it. In this way an executive will be able to make a much more objective judgement on the way forward.

Further reading

The GROW model

Cooper, Robert and Sawaf, Ayman (1998) *Executive EQ – Emotional Intelligence in Business*. Texere Publishing.

Downey, Myles (1999) *Effective Coaching*. Texere Publishing.

Whitmore, Sir John (1996) *Coaching for Performance – Growing People, Performance and Purpose*. Nicholas Brealey.

The coaching spectrum and the suggestion map

Downey, Myles (1999) *Effective Coaching*. Texere Publishing.

Heron, John (1990) *Helping the Client*. Sage.

The skill/will matrix

Landsberg, Max (1997) *The Tao of Coaching*. HarperCollins Business.

Situational Leadership, Center for Leadership Studies, 230 West Third Avenue, Escondido, CA 92025, USA.

The STOP tool

Gallwey, Tim (2002) *The Inner Game of Work*. Texere Publishing.

Feedback

Bee, Roland and Bee, Frances (1998) *Constructive Feedback*. CIPD.

Lucas, Robert (1994) *Coaching Skills – A Guide for Supervisors*. Irwin Professional.

Parsloe, Eric and Wray, Monica (2000) *Coaching and Mentoring – Practical Methods to Improve Learning*. Kogan Page.

Whitmore, Sir John (1996) *Coaching for Performance – Growing People, Performance and Purpose*. Nicholas Brealey.

Working with metaphor and clean language

Cunningham, Ian and Dawes, Graham (1998) *Exercises for Developing Coaching Capability*. CIPD.

Hargrove, Robert (1995) *Masterful Coaching*. Pfeiffer Wiley.

Lawley, James and Tompkins, Penny (2000) *Metaphors in Mind*. Developing Company Press (see: *www.cleanlanguage.co.uk*).

Parkin, Margaret (1998) *Tales for Trainers*. Kogan Page.

Parkin, Margaret (2001) *Tales for Coaching*. Kogan Page.

Team coaching

Katzenbach, Jon R. and Smith, Douglas K. (2003) *Wisdom of Teams: Creating the High-Performance Organization*. HarperBusiness.

Ethics in coaching

Peltier, Bruce (2001) *The Psychology of Executive Coaching.* Brunner-Routledge.

Pilger, John (2003) *New Rulers of the World.* Verso.

Trevino, Linda K. and Nelson, Katherine A. (1995) *Managing Business Ethics.* John Wiley & Sons.

Zeus, P. and Skiffington, S. (2002) *The Coaching at Work Toolkit.* McGraw-Hill Education.

5

Closing the coaching session

Action planning

As Herb Kelleher, CEO of Southwest Airlines, has said: 'We can sit and talk about coaching all day, but at the end of it somebody has got to get up and go and do something and that somebody is you' (Kelleher, 2002). The final part of the face-to-face coaching conversation, the action planning, is absolutely crucial – it's what turns the coaching session through planned activities into final outcomes. In many cases just having a plan of what they are going to do next is the most beneficial thing that the client can ever have. So it is worth spending some time on thinking about how you are going to develop your action planning session. My own logic and theory around this relates to how individuals have seen the problem that they are going to work on. How they see this problem will affect how they see the solution. How they see the solution will affect how they plan their actions. How they plan their actions will affect the outcomes. So it is worth spending some time on how people see the problem.

In many cases I use the metaphor of a map as I believe that this is something that is ingrained into us from early primary school and that we can relate to quite well. If we look at the standard UK school map of the world (see Figure 5.1) you will notice a variety of things about it. However, what you do notice will depend upon your background, your beliefs, your education and possibly some of the heritage of your family. There will be many things that are not immediately apparent – these things are all taken in by the subconscious mind and very often are taken for granted. However, if we look at a traditional US school map of the world (see Figure 5.2) we notice several other things, and because we now have two maps we are able to make a comparison – and it is this comparison that helps bring the subconscious thoughts to the fore. Take a few moments to just to look at the differences between the two.

Had you gone to school in the Pacific Rim or Australia, the traditional map that you would find in schoolrooms is

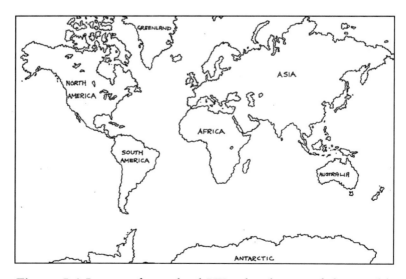

Figure 5.1 Image of standard UK school map of the world.

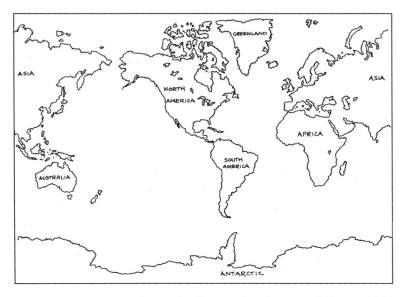

Figure 5.2 Image of standard US school map of the world.

illustrated in Figure 5.3. This gives us even further comparisons and greater cause for confusion and questions about our perceptions and how we see things. Add to this Figure 5.4, which also comes from Australia, and we really start to question things, as well as feel distinctly uncomfortable because things are not looking the way that they always have looked for us.

In Figure 5.5, Arno Peters, the German historian, has taken a projection of the world and portrayed it on a 2D surface to give it a degree of realism that many other maps often overlook – South America is actually nine times larger than Greenland!

So here we have everybody from the same planet, all with their different viewpoints on how they actually see things.

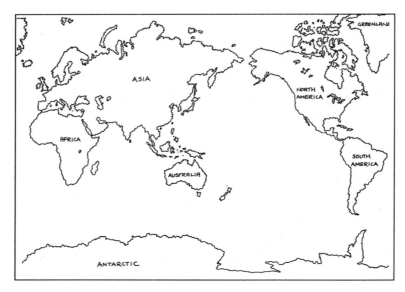

Figure 5.3 Image of standard Pacific Rim or Australian school map of the world.

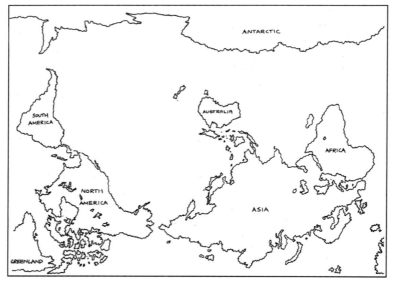

Figure 5.4 Image of Australian 'Down Under' map of the world.

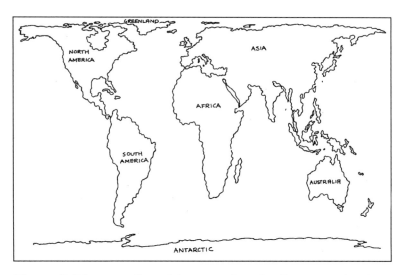

Figure 5.5 Image of world map using the Peters projection.

As has been said before, how you see things will determine how you approach things.

So, as far as action planning is concerned, when coaching someone it is absolutely imperative that we get their view of what is going on, not our view of what they think is going on. It has to be owned and interpreted by the client. In the action planning stage, as one would expect from coaching, there are some very important questions to be asked and after we have the individual's view on the perceived problem this is the time for asking one of those questions: 'What is important here?' This will allow the client to actually dissect the issues and the problems, and pull out what is important, keeping in mind certain factors such as timescales, impact, quality and cost which all should be considered when building up any kind of action plan. It is also important that you challenge the client in terms of what really is important by asking: in what context? how would other people see this? Using the four cornerstones model discussed earlier can help us do just this to ensure that the foundation of the plan is not built in sand but on a rock-solid bed.

Once we have the answer to the question 'What is important here?', the second question 'What do I need to do about it?' is equally applicable. In this particular case what we are looking to do is to start drafting some kind of plan. This may mean that some kind of very loose mind map needs to be put together beforehand, but for the purpose of tracking and following up and to ensure commitment it is usually best if this is written in line with the following points:

- Use positive language.
- Use clear bullet points (such as these).
- Consider timescales.
- Who is actually doing it?
- What is the expected outcome going to be?

Just by following these simple guidelines it is relatively easy and straightforward to draft the semblance of a plan which is not too arduous, is easy to follow, is easy to monitor and is achievable. Once the outline plan has been put together the next step is really to look at the answer to the question 'Who do I need support from?' It is important to identify these people at this stage as support needs to be built into the plan. You may plan on getting support from somebody who might not even be working with your organisation at that point in time or is on holiday. These kinds of issues should be headed off at the pass rather than waiting until you are in the middle of the journey and find yourself derailed.

The final point of the action plan should be to consider how any journey is made. It is not usually a linear process. There are a number of cycles and small eddy currents that spin off from the edge where you have to put one or two extra things in place to make sure you are able to achieve the next part of the journey. The example is often given of an aircraft flying from New York to London which does not fly in a straight line. It has to make numerous corrections on route to account for air currents, wind speed, magnetic deviation and possible rerouting via traffic control – not to mention the mandatory stacking above Heathrow Airport! As such your planning process with your client should take into account all of these factors, and in some cases they may need to take one step back in order to take two forward. If this happens according to plan then it is not such a demotivating factor than if it were to happen out of the blue.

One of the things we tend to build in at the end of a plan is some way of e-mailing it, usually to the coach but it could be to any member of the support team who has been listed in 'Who do I need support from?' above. This adds a commitment to the plan and it also allows the relationship between the coach and the client to be enhanced and helps the coach when they meet up next to ensure that things have progressed that little bit further.

Another factor to consider is that planning very often reduces stress as it does make people believe they are moving in the right direction. However, this is a double-edged sword as sometimes the plan can be so intricate and people get attached to it so much that they have a tendency to use it as a crutch and support mechanism itself. When it gets overused in this way, it then becomes a stress inducer rather than a stress reducer.

Action planning has a tendency to bring the coaching session to a natural close. It also means that you can double back and check to see if you have achieved your goals for the sessions that you have been working on, and if you can factor these into the long-term objectives of the individual and the organisation that the individual is working for, it makes it so much easier to see not only individual growth but the achievement of corporate objectives.

The three D model

This is a classic coaching model where the three Ds stand for: diagnosing, designing and doing. It is a very short, sharp framework that is probably the backbone of most coaching models that are in existence today, such as GROW, skill/will, STOP, etc. The idea is just to get some degree of structure around the whole process of coaching to give a useful platform with some degree of stability that people can then work on. Also, because there is a structure to it, it can be passed from one person to another. One of the many benefits of coaching individuals is that they will take on board your coaching tools and deploy them in an operational context, which is absolutely ideal.

If we consider the three stages, the first, *diagnosing*, can come from many areas. In the executive coaching sense, diagnostics can come from some high-potential toolkit, from psychometric tools, for example the MBTI, or from 360° input from employees within the workplace – or at the very least from some degree of self-assessment. However, if someone is coaching an individual on a particular activity then the diagnosing can start to talk about the following:

- What facts are available to us?
- What other facts do we need?
- Who is the benefactor of this particular piece of work?
- What communication systems are needed to develop this particular piece of work?
- What resources are needed?
- How, once this particular piece of work is finished, will it be put into practice?

Asking the right questions at this stage does ensure clarity and therefore allow a solid foundation built on fact. The key is very often in the questions. On a business trip to Hong Kong with a colleague, I remember seeing quite clearly on the door of the project manager's office of the Mass Transit Railway system in Hong Kong the following notice: 'Do not come in here looking for answers if you have not got the right question!' I also remember the individual whose office it was saying that he believed that statement saved him many hours during the course of the day dealing with individuals who were more than capable of actually thinking for themselves. This is what the diagnosing stage of the three D model is for – to give the individual the opportunity to put on the table all the thoughts, ideas and concepts that they have and in some cases did not know they had so that they can be developed further.

Stage two looks at the *design* and this involves creation and planning. Once again, this should actually be the client's responsibility, not the coach's. Leading on from the diagnostic aspect, a series of questions targeted around what it is we are trying to achieve could help us:

- Who is the benefactor of this piece of work?
- What use is this piece of work going to be put to?
- What else influences this particular piece of work?
- What does this piece of work influence?
- How would our customers benefit from this piece of work?

Usually, in the design stage, it is better to view the project from the end user's point of view rather than the designer's point of view. There are many cases where rectification has to be built onto the end of a process because the designer did not have the foresight to think about who was actually going to use it. The building trade can be a cruel demonstration of this. In a previous career where facilities were being constructed, I remember a significant number of doorways being erected to accommodate wheelchairs, only to find that the actual toilet door itself was the standard size. Had some of these questions been asked in the design stage, things would have been a lot better for the end user.

The last part of the model is the most important part and this is the *doing* stage. As we have seen, Herb Kelleher, the CEO of South West Airlines, has said: 'We can sit and talk about coaching all day, but at the end of it somebody has got to get up and go and do something and that somebody is you.' This is the key point. Many people believe that coaching is a soft, fluffy conversation just used to fill time. This is not my experience. Coaching exists as hard, fast, action-driven conversations that are owned by the client. The coach has permission to guide the client through a series of questions and observations to achieve what they had previously set out. Therefore this part of the three D model should focus on the actual practical actions, with the dates, support mechanisms, timescales and resources that are needed to achieve those actions. It cannot be stressed enough that the doing part of coaching is where it either stands or falls. If you are coaching somebody and you know that follow-up is a particular issue, then you have a responsibility to follow-up yourself on that particular individual. Once the individual client sees that the coach is modelling this particular approach, usually they start to adopt that particular approach themselves.

The other aspect of the doing phase is that when it comes to planning the practical actions, it could mean that you have to revisit the diagnostic stage once again. This is certainly an action I would promote just to double check as this also highlights yet another benefit of coaching. It is in essence a dry run via a conversation of the actual activities that are going to take place and therefore we should make use of all the tools that are available to us at the appropriate times. When we are putting together the plan, i.e. the doing stage, as far as the three D model is concerned, we should go back and review some of the diagnostics, where does this relate to that, etc. This particular tool works well in projects, as these can be introduced as small review cycles in almost any major project cycle. They also work particularly well when learning new skills as you can work through the diagnostic in terms of the teaching material, you can work through the design in terms of the actual lesson plan itself, and then you can use the doing to develop the skills set. Whichever way you use the three D model, if used correctly it can really add an edge to an executive coach's toolkit.

The rule of three

One of the principal concepts of coaching is learning and in order for that to happen a cognitive process needs to take place. Also, we must recognise that in the workplace, habits – both good and bad – are developed.

One bad habit is asking for advice or instruction from managers and not thinking things through for ourselves when we are quite capable of resolving the issue on our own.

Background

There is a two-stage theory (Watkins and Gardiner, 1979) in cognitive psychology which asserts that one aspect of memory structure relies on (1) recall and (2) recognition.

1. Recall involves a search or retrieval process followed by a decision or recognition process based upon the appropriateness of the retrieved information.

2. Recognition involves only the second of these processes.

The theory claims that recall involves two fallible stages whereas recognition involves only one. As a result recognition is superior to recall.

The rule of three

The purpose of the rule of three approach is to give such focus to objectives that the brain is tricked into going straight to recognition, thus avoiding recall. It relies on three questions all are of which are 'Tell me ...' questions.

■ The first is 'Tell me three things about the issue.' This will tell the coach the context of the issue as the client sees it.

■ The second is 'Tell me three consequences ...' Do not elaborate on this by adding anything to the question or it will prompt recall. This informs the coach of the magnitude of the issue.

■ The final question is 'Tell me three things you could do about it.' This is action focused and gives access to a full conversation, if needed, from all the answers given. Also, psychologically the brain has had a 'run up' to the point of action.

Sometimes the client may give you two responses and will follow this by saying 'I can't think of a third.' This is an indication of going into recall. We can get round this by asking, 'If you did know, what would it be?' The absurdity of the question snaps the client out of recall and back into recognition. Picture the scene:

Client: Have you got five minutes?

Coach: Sure what's it about?

Client: The system's down.

Coach: Tell me three things about it.

Client: Well, for one this is the third time this week. Two, complaints are backing up and three, we're going to miss our service level targets if it's not up by tonight.

Coach: OK. And three consequences?

Client: One: miss the bonus this month; two: delayed payments to suppliers; and I can't think if a third.

Coach: If you could what would it be?

Client: Overtime levels up!

Coach: What three things could *we* do about it?

Client: We could check if IT has enough people on the job. We could flag up to customer service about a probable complaints increase.

Coach: And I could alert accounts to contact suppliers.

Client: But what if it keeps going down?

Coach: Let's get this out of the way first, and then we can get our heads together on that one.

Client: OK, thanks.

As illustrated in this example, you may find this approach useful for five-minute impromptu conversations to make them more effective. Another scenario where this tool is useful is in action sessions at the end of training courses.

Why three you may ask? Well, while inexplicable, experience has shown that it has the effect of prompting action and achieving the desired result.

Further reading

Action planning

Cunningham, Ian and Dawes, Graham (1998) *Exercises for Developing Coaching Capability*. CIPD.

Hargrove, Robert (1995) *Masterful Coaching*. Pfeiffer Wiley.

Kelleher, Herb (2002) *The Art of Coaching in Business,* 2nd edn (Video). Greylock Associates.

The three D model

Cunningham, Ian and Dawes, Graham (1998) *Exercises for Developing Coaching Capability*. CIPD.

Hargrove, Robert (1999) *Masterful Coaching*. Pfeiffer Wiley.

The rule of three

Eysenck, M. and Keane, M. (2000) *Cognitive Psychology.* Psychology Press.

6

Evaluating the coaching

Coaching evaluation

Alison Carter, the Director of the European Mentoring and Coaching Council and Head of the IES Coaching Service HR and Training Executives, has identified six areas to be concerned with regarding coaching evaluation.

The first area she highlights for consideration is the audience for the evaluation. She makes a valid point that many people value different things and when setting the aims, objectives and purpose of the evaluation you should make sure that you are clear about whose point of view you are looking at it from. Is it to be from that of the organisation? The department? The individual being coached? HR? The budget holder? Or the programme organiser? As each of these has their own map of reality it is important to establish this from the outset and build it in from the beginning, rather than as an afterthought.

The second area that she points out is the need to define the success criteria before you start to measure. This builds on her previous tip in identifying the key success criteria. Look at what the coaching was designed to do in the first place, pull out from that the success criteria, then look at how you actually measure those criteria. The two primary areas for consideration here would need to be the organisation and the individual and we will look at these later on. It is also worth pointing out at this time that the evaluation actually needs to be explicit as to whose success criteria and whose outcomes it seeks to measure. It is also worth mentioning that the key success criteria that we are considering here are not those of the individual getting coached as this aspect is usually covered in the individual's contract with the coach. The success criteria here are more in relation to the commissioning of the coaching.

The third area Alison points out is the need to plan ahead and get the coaches to collect the data for you. It is absolutely crucial that this is woven into the contract with the individual, as the content of the coaching conversations is confidential. Most coaches have their own ways of evaluating their performance and that of those they are coaching, and helping the individuals to identify and evaluate their own success from the coaching. It may be that you get a one-page evaluation from the client you are coaching at the end of the contract. It may be that you take five minutes just to jot down some notes from their comments at the end of each session. Either way, you should build up some form of evaluative journal.

Point number four states that you should not just rely on what the individual being coached tells you. It is fair to say that most individuals will give you a very subjective overview of what has worked for them and, by and large, most of them say that coaching is favourably received. But what we need here is a balanced approach rather than just one point of view and as such it is useful if you can get some form of 360° or reverse feedback mechanism working in this area. This way you are working more with the impact rather than the outcome of the coaching.

Tip number five is extremely useful as it relates to getting feedback on processes you can change the next time, but it also highlights a point in setting up the key success criteria. Is the individual being coached looking to develop further individuals or looking to expedite a process or procedure? The individual should be able to identify which part of the process or procedure they can have most impact on, similarly with individuals and where they can have most impact. By projecting this forward to the future you should also be able to get feedback on processes that you the coach can change about your approach the next time you actually coach that individual.

Point number six fires a warning shot across the bows of most finance departments because it highlights the dangers of being wed to magic formulas. Most of these are based around value or return on investment (ROI). This looks at ROI in percentage terms as follows:

$$\text{ROI } (\%) = \frac{\text{Benefit } (\pounds/\text{€}/\$) - \text{Cost of coaching} \times 100}{\text{Cost of coaching}}$$

The key area to consider here is how to estimate the benefit data. It is fair to say that the closer to the till the individual is the easier it is to work out, as can be seen from the example given in the section on bottom line benefits below.

Paul Kearns and Tony Miller were the authors of a Financial Times Management Briefing entitled *Measuring the Impact of Training and Development on the Bottom Line*. In this briefing they put together what they referred to as a KPMT added value model and I have adapted this on several occasions to look at how we evaluate coaching. Their model works over five levels:

- Base level – baseline business measures.
- Level 1 – reaction to the coaching.
- Level 2 – learning.
- Level 3 – impact on the workplace or behaviour.
- Level 4 – bottom-line added value, measured in relation to the base level measures taken.

Consequently, this model is all about measuring added value, which is what many people are looking for. The model itself works on the premise that there must be clear business objectives for which there is already a baseline and this is the first level – a bottom-line measure. In essence they are looking to improve that particular measure through the coaching, and the evaluation of the coaching is by re-measuring the progress towards that objective during the process and after the coaching is completed. In summary, it highlights whether or not the coaching is actually adding any value. Added value comes from a combination of the four values listed in Figure 6.1.

The box on the left represents the value of the organisation which an accountant would be able to calculate – including even a sum to cover goodwill. The basic proposition for the coaching is whether the box gets bigger as a result of the coaching investment. If it does not

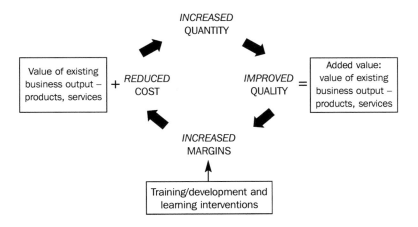

Figure 6.1 Added value can only come from a combination of these four values.

then the coaching cannot be said to be adding value and from an organisational point of view is questionable as to whether it is worthwhile.

Interestingly enough, if you want to add value to the organisation there are a few key variables which you can influence that will result in added value, such as outputs, costs, prices and margins. Improving quality also has to be included as improved quality feeds through to customer perceptions and results in more products or services being demanded. Kearns and Miller (1997) have actually taken it to the next stage by asking the questions listed below in their nine-step added-value evaluation model.

- *Step 1* – What business output measures are you trying to improve?

- *Step 2* – Who has an impact on these outputs and by how much?

- *Step 3* – Can their impact be improved through coaching interventions?

- *Step 4* – What bottom-line 'tell-tales' can be used to measure small improvements?

- *Step 5* – What coaching objectives can deliver the required improvements?

- *Step 6* – How are the participants reacting to the coaching input?

- *Step 7* – Are they developing where they are meant to be developing?

- *Step 8* – Are they using the learning at work?

- *Step 9* – Has the intervention had the desired effect on the business output measures?

It is fair to say that this is one of the most comprehensive forms of evaluation that you are likely to come across as it views coaching not as a cost but as an added value – which is where most coaches would want it to be. It should be said that Kearns and Miller hold that if a business objective cannot be cited as a basis for coaching then no coaching should be offered. This is one area I disagree with as coaching has now taken on a wider perspective in terms of life skills, and in the stress-laden environment of the workplace that we operate in today, coaching can be offered for personal development that is not aligned with business objectives. In some cases individuals can be coached to the point of leaving the organisation – which one could contend represents a business benefit! (Although this may sometimes be hard to believe, it's not the first time I have heard this argument.) This leads us onto our next area and revisits a traditional triangulation approach to evaluation.

There are predominantly two ways to evaluate something:

1. *Quantitatively* – which has some degree of numbers or measurement attached to it.

2. *Qualitatively* – which usually includes things like anecdotal evidence, feel-good factors and subjective comments.

The triangulation approach uses two of one and one of the other in any combination. Therefore what you would end up with is possibly one measurement which looks at hard and fast numbers (quantitative) and two subjective aspects, such as a learning log and testimonies from clients (qualitative). By using this approach – which in many cases was honed during the early years of Investors in People in the United Kingdom – one can at least give due diligence to the process of evaluation. As has been mentioned before, this should be built in at the start rather than afterwards.

Donald Kirkpatrick developed a four-stage model back in 1959 consisting of the following components:

- *Level 1* – reaction.
- *Level 2* – learning.
- *Level 3* – transfer of behaviour.
- *Level 4* – organisational benefits.

Although one can immediately see that traditional methods of evaluation, such as Kirkpatrick's, which work on four levels need some degree of adaptation to work in the coaching environment, there is no problem in having four levels of evaluation along the following lines:

- *Level 1* – identifying and evaluating clear business benefits.
- *Level 2* – impact of coaching on the individual (client).
- *Level 3* – transfer of impact to wider audience (team?).
- *Level 4* – organisational benefits.

Through this slight adaptation one can see that it can be developed further and produce quite a useful model for evaluation.

Bottom-line benefits

As mentioned earlier, the 'closer to the till' the individual is the easier it is to evaluate the benefits. When Tony Morgan, the then CEO of the Industrial Society (IS), first introduced me to coaching he asked me to lead a sales coaching project. This involved myself and two other very good sales people, Tony Bolton and Kate Matheson. Tony lived quite close to Birmingham, Kate lived in Yorkshire and I lived in Scotland. Our target audience came from across the United Kingdom in the IS offices.

We set up five key criteria as follows:

- Coaching had to be called for by the client, not imposed by the management.
- We would not coach anyone who was currently in a disciplinary process.
- We would not coach anyone from our own office. (I would not coach anyone from Glasgow, Tony from Birmingham or Kate from Leeds.)
- Targets would be set by the clients themselves.
- Only the expenses would be charged to the project budget, not the time of the three coaches.

The three coaches also had a responsibility to hit their own sales targets during the project.

No fewer than 12 people requested coaching from the Society's five offices and the three coaches set up contracts with all 12 for an initial period of 12 months.

As a sales person is 'close to the till' in an organisational process it was fairly straightforward to set up the objectives, targets and drivers for the project. Each sales person had a sales target (x) and each coach negotiated a coaching target, which in some cases was greater than x and in some cases lower. The lower targets were usually set due to unrealistic performance targets having already been set and a more achievable target was needed to give the sales person motivation, inspiration and hope!

It was agreed with the heads of department that we would not count sales figures as 'impacts of coaching' until individuals had hit the targets that the respective heads of department had set them.

The following facts and figures are the results of the 12 months of coaching with all 12 people. The project actually ran for 14 months in total and was then rolled out to various regions. (I have not mentioned any names, individual targets or circumstances in this example.)

- Taking the 12 sales targets set for the 12 months gave us a total of £765,000. Not everyone had the same target.
- After 12 months only two people failed to hit their original sales target. Everyone hit his or her coaching target.
- The total amount generated over and above the original £765,000 was £525,000, making the total sales revenue for the 12 months of £1,290,000.

This was the first quantitative approach to the evaluation.

- We had the sales team talk at various meetings to give testimony to our approach and generally promote coaching throughout our organisation

This was the qualitative method.

- We generated two known sales contracts with a total sales value of £56,000 for the IS as a direct result of having a coach in attendance with the sales person on sales visits.

This was the second quantitative approach that was used.

If we look at the cost involved of moving myself, Tony and Kate around the country for the project it amounted to £14,762.

By using the triangulation approach to evaluation, we had a clean evaluation of the project that was audited by the accounts department and approved by them. Interestingly enough some of the heads of department who set the original sales targets still questioned the outcome!

What is beyond question, however, is that, during that year, the people on the project, both coaches and clients, had more fun, job satisfaction and a feeling of contribution than they had ever had before.

It is also worth mentioning that, as was par for the course, the three coaches hit their own targets with room to spare.

Further reading

Kearns, P. and Miller, T. (1997) *Measuring the Impact of Training and Development on the Bottom Line*. Financial Times Prentice Hall.

Tamkin, P., Yarnell, J. and Kerrin, M. (2002) *Kirkpatrick and Beyond*, Institute for Employment Studies Report No. 392. Available from: *http:www.employment-studies.co.uk*

Training Journal Focus Supplement, January 2004. Available at: *www.trainingjournal.com*.

7

Conclusion

CPD and supervision

With the advent of professional standards in the field of coaching there is a constant drive for continuous professional development and supervision. The supervision here is meant in the clinical sense, rather than in the leadership sense. It allows coaches to develop themselves through active and passive methods of engagement and reflection. This aspect of qualification has also had an influence – it is all very well being qualified, but how current is the qualification? Certainly, in the world of coaching, one is looking for the most current qualification that is available. Most purchasers of executive coaching or coaching services are therefore looking for coaching organisations and coaches that are constantly reinventing themselves and developing themselves in a professional manner.

There are many aspects to continuing professional development (CPD) and the best place to start is with yourself. A regular audit of your approaches, behaviours and attributes along the coaching spectrum needs to be carried out and subsequent action plans developed from it.

Such things as learning styles, Myers Briggs Type Indicators and coaching competency questionnaires with 360° feedback are useful ways of getting objective information and analysis carried out on yourself. This should form the crux of any CPD programme.

The second area to consider is the amount of knowledge that has been developed in the coaching field. You need to be diligent with regard to knowledge acquisition, whether this be through reading publications, articles, journals or books, viewing videos or DVDs on appropriate subjects or visiting websites (although some websites leave a lot to be desired) – it all helps to acquire knowledge in the field of coaching. Keep in mind that if your learning style is one of reflection you need to record all this in a way that allows you to reflect on the knowledge acquired.

The third area to consider is one of skill deployment. It is all very well having the knowledge; however, the skills need to be practised and honed. One of the best ways of doing this is to write up the coaching sessions that you undertake. It is important to keep in mind the confidentiality aspect, so when writing these notes up for a CPD purpose you should refer to the context and not the content of the coaching sessions. It is good practice to finish most coaching sessions by asking if there is anything that could have been done differently, just to get immediate feedback from the client – this is very useful in terms of one's own CPD.

The next area to consider is the kind of networks that you take part in. Networks are becoming more commonplace in the UK and we are now finding more and more network meetings springing up. The Oxford School of Coaching and

Mentoring has local network meetings around various parts of the country. Peter McKechnie of Phoenix Coaching provides a number of networks across Scotland and supplies regular inputs on regular themes that allow coaches to get together and discuss various issues. Pauline Willis and Anna Britnor Guest of the Coaching and Mentoring Network run virtual networks that one can log on to and discuss a variety of issues on their extensive forums. Despite earlier comments, this is one of the better websites as it is constantly being updated and is full of valuable information for the coach.

On an annual basis the CPD should be reviewed by a competent member of the coaching fraternity. This usually involves reviewing evidence that is submitted in whatever format, whether electronically or paper-based, and having a face-to-face discussion with a coach just to establish where the key learning has been from the previous year and what is happening in the coming year that the coach is likely to want to develop further. Personally speaking, I would maintain that a CPD approach is mandatory, given the area in which we are working which can be fraught with danger, and given the pace of change within the field of coaching. In any event, it is vital that coaches keep up to date with what is current and accurate in today's marketplace.

Another area to consider is that of supervision, in a clinical sense as mentioned previously rather than in the leadership sense. This has two benefits: it allows coaches to co-coach each other and thus can add to the continuing professional development, but it can also allow coaches to untangle some of the ethical dilemmas that arise during coaching sessions. While this does have a therapeutic effect, as you will have found out from this book, coaching is not about therapy – it is about being proactive and therefore can be therapeutic. Supervision itself should form part of any continuing development programme as it taps into the predominant learning style each of us has and allows us to reflect on it in such a way that we can develop our expertise for the future. Also, as mentioned above, if there is any baggage around in the form of ethical dilemmas, these can literally be opened up on this platform, investigated, dissected, categorised, tidied up and put away again, to use a psychological metaphor.

To this end the European Mentoring and Coaching Council offers this advice on the qualities to look for in selecting a supervisor:

- They have experience as a coach/mentor.
- They have experience of being supervised.
- They have experience as a supervisor (not necessarily of coaches/mentors).
- They evidence a theoretical framework for their own practice and you find this relevant to your own work.
- They evidence theoretical framework(s) relating to supervision.
- They have an understanding of the context of coaching/ mentoring (as practised by the supervisee).
- They are aware of the impact of values, beliefs and assumptions (of the supervisor or coach/mentor in their own practice).

- They are respectful of diversity in its many forms and alert to its potential benefits and pitfalls.

- They demonstrate a capacity for self-regulation (and will need to foster this in the supervisee).

- They show commitment to CPD for themselves and others.

- They agree to abide by the EMCC Code of Ethics, even if not an EMCC member.

- There will be no dual roles (i.e. the supervisor is not also the line manager, business partner, etc. although peer supervision is acceptable, e.g. between colleagues, students).

Many organisations that have qualified coaches in their ranks as a result of attending coaching courses now have continuing professional development programmes running alongside. In some cases this actually facilitates a licensing approach that is granted by the organisation. Anne Welsh of People Development within Standard Life has developed one such programme over the past few years and now a has a batch of some 17 coaches that regularly attend CPD events, facilitate coaching clubs within the organisation, have a licence to coach throughout all departments of Standard Life and run electronic forums and networks, as well as attending outside events and thus promoting Standard Life's approach to people development. It has not, I am sure Anne would be the first to admit, been an easy task for her but certainly the result is a quality product that gives due respect to the process of continuing professional development.

Conclusions

It is always interesting when you try and draw some conclusions from the work you have been doing, the notes you have taken, the writing that has been scribbled down on numerous bits of paper. It forces us to look into where things have come from, to make sense of them in today's world and to look at where they could go in the future. I recall two tales regarding great sports coaches in the past of meetings they had with their teams. According to one story, the coach simply put the ball down on the ground in front of the goal, pointed to the ball and said 'ball', pointed to the goal and said 'target', and then kicked the ball with such a degree of venom that it hit the back of the net. His comment then was: 'That is what you have got to do.' In the other story the coach merely informed the team that the transport would be leaving for the away ground at one o'clock outside the main stand!

So, on a sports front, we can see that things have come a very long way. On the business front, recent findings from a CIPD survey of 500 of its members show us that coaching is very much on the up, as revealed by the following statistics:

- 99 per cent agree that coaching can deliver tangible benefits to both individuals and organisations.
- 93 per cent agree that coaching and mentoring are key mechanisms for transferring learning from training courses back to the workplace.

- 92 per cent agree that when coaching is managed effectively it can have a positive impact on the bottom line.
- 96 per cent agree that coaching is an effective way to promote learning in organisations

However, there is still a long way to go:

- 60 per cent of respondents claim to have no formal written strategy for the coaching activities taking place in their organisation.
- Only 5 per cent claim to have all line managers trained to coach their team members.
- Only 14 per cent claim that coaching skills training is compulsory for all staff who manage people.
- Only 3 per cent claim to use assessment against objectives set at the start of a coaching initiative as the basis for evaluating success.

So where is coaching now? Well, on the qualifications front there are eleven awarding bodies in the United Kingdom, with various qualifications ranging from entry-level through postgraduate and onto masters, whereas back in 1998 the Industrial Society's joint venture with Myles Downey in the School of Coaching was to become the first and only UK university qualification in the field of business coaching. We have also seen a shift from coaching being used as an extension of on-the-job training in the workplace to the point where it has now become very context-specific, ranging from the traditional to the transitional, from coaching somebody through a shift in post to transformational, high-performance coaching that enables people to see things with a completely different mindset and then go on to even greater achievements.

To a certain extent part of this background is a result of sports coaching. We have seen the change in the stature and physique of Olympic sprinters as a result of their desire to move their upper limbs faster – Linford Christie's long held belief that the faster you move the upper limbs, the faster you can move the lower ones certainly held him in good stead and has seen the coaching world thrown wide open. However, it is not uncommon to find that the coach has no prior knowledge of the particular discipline that they are currently working in. Indeed, some would say that it is easier to be non-directive than directive if you have no prior knowledge of the area that you want to work in.

We can see that sport has passed on its discoveries to the world of business coaching, and we can also see that there is a significant number of coaches now coming onto the global marketplace. This in turn brings its own problems. Coaching, by its very nature, has been self-regulating in the past. People enjoy the free spirit that is often regarded as necessary in the area of non-directive coaching, so how can you tie this area down with bureaucracy and standards? This is something that has been wrestled with by the great and the good in the world of coaching for many years. The European Council of Coaching and Mentoring is in the process of putting together a set of standards for the UK and Europe. The International Coaching Federation has its own standards and code of ethics that many believe have served it well in the past. However, as coaching is becoming more global it is understandable that people want to put their own interpretation and develop these areas further. It also makes it interesting from the point of view of qualifications – who is to say that the frameworks and the qualifications that any of the universities or the Awarding Bodies in the United Kingdom put together are in fact appropriate? There is nobody to universally preside over the process of establishing a set of standards. This is something that the world of coaching needs – and needs much sooner rather than later.

It is also interesting to note in this conclusion where coaching is used the most in the workplace. Managing change seems to be the most popular application as it can be coached on any of the areas that can be missing in the change process. It is usually a given that for change to occur the process shown in Figure 7.1 has to happen. However, coaching can be used to facilitate the filling in of any gaps which would otherwise prevent change (see Figure 7.2), very often by using the models that are covered in this book.

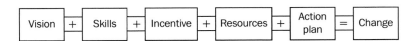

Figure 7.1 The change process.

Another area where coaching seems to be frequently used in the workplace is performance management. It is a natural step to run a performance management process through interviews such as appraisals by using a coaching style. It helps develop the conversation, builds trust and gives focused outputs.

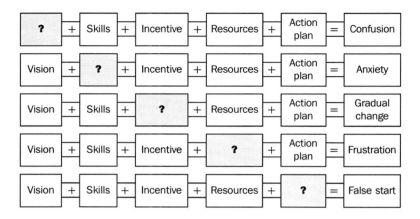

Figure 7.2 Filling in the gaps preventing change.

Leadership style is also an interesting application for coaching. My own view is that coaching is more aligned to leadership than it is to management as it is more of a people process. Taking a leadership approach of appreciative enquiry and developing your coaching style, in my experience, has a tendency to get more out of the team and more out of yourself in terms of enjoyment and contribution.

Coaching has also long been used in terms of training and a rethink is now due in this area. Given that we now have more coaches out in the workplace, should we not be using these more to reinforce some of the training programmes that people have actually been on? There is a big need in the market literally to coordinate their training and coaching approaches by way of actually transferring learning to the workplace.

A further area in which we have seen coaching used in the world of work is in recruitment. While this area is in its infancy, people are now beginning to realise that managers are starting to coach their staff and therefore we now see coaching exercises on many development centre approaches to recruitment.

It would be remiss of me to put a book together such as this without looking at why coaching does not always work. I expect many of you will be looking at this book expecting this area to be touched on only to be disappointed to find where the answers lie. From an organisational point of view, trying to drive in a 'uniform coaching culture' across all departments will not work. As I have said, we all have different maps and therefore all have different ways of doing things. Approaching each department, section or team on an individual basis will help, as will giving consideration to the areas mentioned in Figure. 7.2 above. On an individual basis, the fault can only lie with two people: either the coach or the client. It very often requires some pretty deep and honest soul-searching to establish which of the two is at fault, or indeed both. It has to be said, from my experience, that in only one case is it the client's fault and this is the obvious one where the client simply does not want to be coached. In such a case neither you nor I nor anyone else for that matter is going to coach that particular client. The client has to come to the conclusion for themselves that coaching is what they want, and it is interesting to see how this little game is played out in the workplace. If you think of this logically – and I have seen this on many occasions – there is an absolute shift very, very quickly to realisation of what is required. It goes along the following lines:

A manager has problems with an individual who is not hitting performance targets and during the process of performance management confronts the issue with the individual. The individual has been with the organisation for some length of time, is very set in their ways and does not want to move on. They think that the organisation should actually revolve around them. So the manager highlights the difficulty to the individual and then offers the individual a degree of coaching, explaining what coaching is and how it works. The individual replies along the following lines: 'I don't want any of that coaching nonsense.' So the next step is for the manager to offer a degree of training. To which the individual says: 'I've been there before, I've done that course, I could run that course myself.'

It is at this point that the manager should realise his or her responsibilities as a manager, not as a coach. There has been no agreement from the individual with regard to coaching and therefore the only option the manager has is to manage.

If this approach is taken the manager then has access to numerous tools. For example, you have an individual that is underperforming, you have offered coaching and it has been rejected, you have offered training and it has been rejected, so the only other route to go down is discipline (a management tool), though it is my experience that this is contrary to the culture in many organisations. However, the fact of the matter is you have an individual working for you that does not want to be trained, does not want to be coached and is still not reaching the performance criteria.

Therefore you have to use the appropriate tools and techniques, and as such discipline to get somebody up to the level required by the organisation is the route that should be taken. Remember, as we said before, coaching is not an easy option and neither is management. If the individual still refuses then you have to go down the discipline route. By the same standards the individual has the option to take out a grievance if they wish and that would be dealt with in due process. However, when confronted with this, my experience is that the individual usually would like to try some coaching, but the question is, 'Have they bought into it for the right reasons?' This leads us now onto some of the reasons why coaching won't work because the fault lies with the coach.

One of the areas that I have highlighted already in the book, in the section on the skill/will matrix in Chapter 4, is taking the wrong approach. The individual might need a direct approach but you take a guiding approach and therefore coaching will not work in the style that you have deployed it. It is important that you match your particular coaching style to the needs and desires of the individual that you are coaching. If somebody is fully skilled but de-motivated, no number of training courses on the particular issue would get them motivated to reach the target that they need to achieve. So ensure you approach the coaching using the right style.

The third area is one that actually arises between the coach and the client, that is where there is a lack of trust between them. Sometimes you find that the coach does not actually trust the client to do what they said they were going to do and sometimes the client actually believes the coach is a management spy. With this lack of trust the coaching collapses. On many occasions, on many training courses, I have had many people take away the key learning point from the first session that if coaching trust does not exist, coaching just will not happen.

That leads us onto the area we touched on in the section on action planning which is the client's perception of the coach. Sometimes a coach may have a low 'coaching rateable value' (CRV) which is usually an indication that they have coached somebody who has passed on by word of mouth that that coach does come up to expectation. As a result other people are then reluctant to be coached by that particular individual. Each coach has a responsibility to develop their own CRV and using the tools and techniques in this book can help you achieve this. Giving due diligence to your own development, constantly checking your degree of competence and building up a track record as someone who is very good and professional in their approach will increase your CRV. If these areas are given the proper level of attention you will find that coaching has a tendency to work rather than not, but it is not a panacea. Use it appropriately, and when called to, be committed to it.

The future

So what does the future hold for coaching? Well one thing is for sure, there are more and more coaches coming onto the market – life coaches, work–life balance coaches, business coaches, executive coaches. People from the world of counselling are coming over into coaching and there are people that are qualified consultants that are now finding that coaching skills are useful as an addition to their consultancy skills. Given that there are more people coming in, it should be the case that there is more high-quality coaching going on. However, this does not always follow and there are two areas of concern in today's world.

As previously mentioned, the EMCC is developing standards which should very shortly be published, standards the industry is crying out for, especially given the intake mentioned above. A further area that needs to be considered in a similar vein is some kind of framework for the qualifications available. Purchasers of these qualifications are continually asking how one qualification fits in with another. Just recently in the United Kingdom the standards among qualifications have been thrown into the air and brought back down to earth again in a uniform fashion by the requirement that all qualifications that attract government funding fit into the National Vocational Qualification framework. Indeed Europe has also adopted a uniform approach so that by the year 2010 all standards for qualifications have to fit into the framework set up by the Bologna Agreement. The Scottish Credit and Qualifications Framework (SQCF) has developed a ready-reckoner to illustrate how qualifications such as HNCs, HNDs, postgraduate certificates, diplomas, etc. fit into the standardised framework that the Bologna Agreement is steering all of Europe towards by the year 2010 (see Appendix 3). This could be seen as an extension of the standards mentioned earlier or it could be a stand-alone piece of work. However, one thing is for sure – the industry requires it.

The other concern I have is the fees that coaching attracts. In many cases, I have no problems or concerns with some of the major players in executive coaching and the fees that they demand. Where I do have problems is when individuals who have left organisations, have no track record and have no benchmarking set themselves up as coaches and charge extortionate prices. Such fees ultimately are not value for money as many of the individuals involved lack focus and do not supply a quality product. Every industry has individuals of this nature that enter it so it would seem sensible that, in conjunction with the standards, there should be some form of register to ensure that coaches operating in the world of business coaching and/or life coaching are covered by the appropriate back-up and support systems such as CPD, supervision and insurance.

All this leads us to believe that there is an interesting time ahead in the field of coaching. This conclusion may apply primarily to the coaches themselves rather than the clients. From the client's perspective coaching certainly offers an answer to the question: 'What do you want to be when you grow up?' From a reactive perspective it can also help you get over the issue of climbing the ladder of success only to find out the ladder has been leaning against the wrong wall and – to add insult to injury – now that you are at the top of the ladder you find out you suffer from vertigo. So my advice in my concluding remarks is for you to find a coach that you trust, be committed, be inspired and get your life back. It is not a case of what have you got to loose, it is more a case of what you can achieve.

The European Mentoring and Coaching Council Code of Ethics

Introduction

The European Mentoring and Coaching Council (EMCC) has been established to promote best practice and ensure that the highest possible standards are maintained in the coach/mentoring relationship, whatever form that might take, so that the coach/mentoring environment provides the greatest opportunity for learning and development.

Purpose

This Ethical Code sets out what the clients and sponsors can expect from the coach/mentor in either a coach/mentoring, training or supervisory relationship and should form the starting point for any contract agreed. All members of the EMCC accept the principles and aims of the EMCC. We recognise that members may not always maintain these ethical principles. The EMCC has therefore agreed a process by which breaches of the Code by a member can be reported and investigated. This is referred to later in this document.

All EMCC members will make the sponsoring organisation and the individual client aware, at the contracting stage, of the existence of the Code of Ethics.

Terminology

The term 'coach/mentoring' is used to describe all types of coaching or mentoring that may be taking place, both in the work environment and outside. The EMCC recognises that there will be many types of coach/mentoring taking place and these will need to be defined when more detailed standards are produced. The term 'client' denotes anyone using the services of a coach/mentor. We believe the term 'client' is interchangeable with any other term that the parties to the coach/mentoring relationship might be more comfortable with, such as 'colleague', 'learner', 'partner', 'coachee' or 'mentee'. It is recognised that there are circumstances where the coach/mentor may have two 'clients', the individual being coached and the organisation who may have commissioned the coach/mentoring. In this Code we have used the term 'sponsor' to differentiate the latter. The terms 'supervision' and 'supervisor' describe the process by which the work of the coach/mentor is overseen and advice/guidance sought. The terminology is the same, but the process may differ in significant ways from that undertaken in other professions, such as psychotherapy and counselling.

The Code

The coach/mentor will acknowledge the dignity of all humanity. They will conduct themselves in a way which respects diversity and promotes equal opportunities. It is the primary responsibility of the coach/mentor to provide the best possible service to the client and to act in such a way as to cause no harm to any client or sponsor. The coach/ mentor is committed to functioning from a position of dignity, autonomy and personal responsibility. The EMCC Ethical Code covers the following:

- Competence
- Context
- Boundary management
- Integrity
- Professionalism.

Competence

1. The coach/mentor will:

    (a) Ensure that their level of experience and know-ledge is sufficient to meet the needs of the client.

    (b) Ensure that their capability is sufficient to enable them to operate according to this Code of Ethics and any standards that may subsequently be produced.

    (c) Develop and then enhance their level of compe-tence by participating in relevant training and appropriate Continuing Professional Development activities.

(d) Maintain a relationship with a suitably qualified supervisor, who will regularly assess their competence and support their development. The supervisor will be bound by the requirements of confidentiality referred to in this Code. What constitutes a 'suitably qualified' supervisor is defined in the EMCC's standards document.

Context

2. The coach/mentor will:

(a) Understand and ensure that the coach/mentoring relationship reflects the context within which the coach/mentoring is taking place.

(b) Ensure that the expectations of the client and the sponsor are understood and that they themselves understand how those expectations are to be met.

(c) Seek to create an environment in which client, coach/mentor and sponsor are focused on and have the opportunity for learning.

Boundary management

3. The coach/mentor will:

(a) At all times operate within the limits of their own competence, recognise where that competence has the potential to be exceeded and where necessary refer the client either to a more experienced coach/mentor, or support the client in seeking the help of another professional, such as a counsellor, psychotherapist or business/financial advisor.

(b)   Be aware of the potential for conflicts of interest of either a commercial or emotional nature to arise through the coach/mentoring relationship and deal with them quickly and effectively to ensure there is no detriment to the client or sponsor.

Integrity

4.   The coach/mentor will:

(a)   Maintain throughout the level of confidentiality which is appropriate and is agreed at the start of the relationship.

(b)   Disclose information only where explicitly agreed with the client and sponsor (where one exists), unless the coach/mentor believes that there is convincing evidence of serious danger to the client or others if the information is withheld.

(c)   Act within applicable law and not encourage, assist or collude with others engaged in conduct which is dishonest, unlawful, unprofessional or discriminatory.

Professionalism

5.   The coach/mentor will:

(a)   Respond to the client's learning and development needs as defined by the agenda brought to the coach/mentoring relationship.

(b)   Not exploit the client in any manner, including, but not limited to, financial, sexual or those matters within the professional relationship. The coach/mentor will ensure that the duration of the coach/mentoring contract is only as long as is necessary for the client/sponsor.

(c)   Understand that professional responsibilities continue beyond the termination of any coach/mentoring relationship. These include the following:

–   Maintenance of agreed confidentiality of all information relating to clients and sponsors.

–   Avoidance of any exploitation of the former relationship.

–   Provision of any follow-up which has been agreed to.

–   Safe and secure maintenance of all related records and data.

(d)   Demonstrate respect for the variety of different approaches to coaching and mentoring and other individuals in the profession.

(e)   Never represent the work and views of others as their own.

(f)   Ensure that any claim of professional competence, qualifications or accreditation is clearly and accurately explained to potential clients and that no false or misleading claims are made or implied in any published material.

Breaches of the Code

EMCC members will at all times represent coaching and mentoring in a way which reflects positively on the profession. Where a client or sponsor believes that a member of the EMCC has acted in a way which is in breach of this Ethical Code, they should first raise the matter and seek resolution with the member concerned. Either party can ask the EMCC to assist in the process of achieving resolution. If the client or sponsor remains unsatisfied they are entitled to make a formal complaint. Complaints will be dealt with according to the EMCC's 'Complaints and Disciplinary Procedure'. EMCC members will provide a copy of this document upon request. A copy can be obtained by writing to:

European Mentoring & Coaching Council
Sherwood House
7 Oxhey Road
Watford
Hertfordshire WD19 4QF

or e-mail: *info@emccouncil.org*

In the event that a complaint should be made against an EMCC member, that member must cooperate in resolving such a complaint. EMCC members will confront a colleague when they have reasonable cause to believe they are acting in an unethical manner and, failing resolution, will report that colleague to the EMCC.

Coaching competencies and associated behaviours

The coach:

- respects the uniqueness of others;
- uses the full range of approaches from directive to non-directive;
- acts out of the belief that every person has huge unlimited potential;
- creates partnerships with their learners;
- displays openness, honesty, empathy, integrity and a passion for individual learning and development, both personal and professional.

In order for a coach to be effective they must be competent. There are four stages of competence:

Stage 1 – Unconscious incompetence

Stage 2 – Conscious incompetence

Stage 3 – Unconscious competence

Stage 4 – Conscious competence

The following core competencies are aimed at getting the coach to Stage 4 by illustrating the behaviours that are expected of an effective coach.

Competencies

Coaching is the art of facilitating the development, learning and enhanced performance of another. Outlined below are ten key coaching competencies and their associated behaviours.

1. Initiating the coaching relationship

- Ensures that coaching meetings take place uninterrupted in appropriate surroundings at a mutually convenient time.
- Puts others at ease by use of the appropriate actions, language and behaviours.
- Gives another undivided attention.
- Demonstrates strong belief in the boundless potential of others.
- Demonstrates strength of personal commitment to learning and development.
- Establishes the parameters of a relationship built on mutual respect.
- Establishes trust.
- Demonstrates integrity.

2. Developing the coaching relationship

- Shows sensitivity to the needs, feelings, moods and emotions of others.

- Is easily accessible.
- Responds speedily to requests for contact/support.
- Confronts negative behaviours and attitudes.
- Offers feedback with recipient's permission.
- Can be relied upon to offer appropriate and objective feedback.
- Is consistently creative in approach to others.

3. Managing self

Self-awareness

- Suspends judgement to achieve maximum objectivity in one's relations with others.
- Works in the full knowledge of one's own set of values, beliefs, prejudices, emotions and preferences.

Controlling emotions and stress

- Handles the emotions of others without becoming personally involved.
- Remains calm in difficult situations or when faced with uncertainty.
- Accepts personal feedback or criticism without becoming defensive.
- Responds honestly to other's emotions.
- Confronts conflict objectively and honestly.

Managing continuing personal learning and development

- Takes responsibility for meeting own learning and development needs.
- Seeks feedback on own performance to identify strengths and weaknesses.
- Modifies behaviour wherever needed as a result of feedback.
- Reflects systematically on own performance in order to improve it.
- Develops self to meet changing/new demands.
- Transfers learning from one situation to another.

4. Working within an agreed ethical code

- Manages their own personal values, attitudes and beliefs.
- Agrees a clear code of practice/contract for the coaching relationship.
- Recognises and explains limits of own competence.
- Gives clear, relevant and timely information on sources of additional support.
- Clearly identifies and raises ethical issues.
- Confronts and works towards the resolution of ethical dilemmas.
- Confronts discriminatory attitudes and behaviours.

5. *Working with a set of beliefs*

- Clearly and candidly manages one's own values, attitudes, beliefs and emotions when appropriate.
- Displays empathy – the ability to enter imaginatively into and understand another's values, attitudes, beliefs and emotions but remain neutral and non-judgemental.
- Demonstrates a non-judgemental acceptance of others.
- Works in the expectation of mutual respect.

6. *Communicating*

Listening to understand

- Demonstrates active listening by asking questions, seeking clarification, rephrasing others' statements and summarising to check understanding.
- Uses positive body language and non-verbal signals to demonstrate openness and undivided attention.
- Confirms understanding through observation and interpretation of non-verbal signals (body language, facial expression, tone, vocal signals).
- Listens to understand motivation.
- Listens to pick up emotions.
- Makes appropriate use of silence.

Promoting understanding

- Presents ideas and information in ways which are easily understood.
- Uses styles of communication that are appropriate to listeners and situations, including choice of time and place.
- Seeks to clarify the understanding of others.
- Encourages listeners to ask questions.
- Paraphrases and summarises to promote understanding.
- Modifies communication methods and style in response to feedback.
- Recognises and expresses emotions.
- Responds appropriately to others' emotions.

7.   *Focusing on goals*

- Enables another to identify their goals.
- Enables another to clarify and refine their goals.
- Challenges assumptions and unfocused thinking.
- Enables another to achieve a clearly imagined vision of how it will be/feel when the goal is achieved.
- Challenges change or loss of focus.
- Overcomes distractions.
- Uses feedback to maintain clarity of vision and purpose.

8. Striving for excellence

- Creates a personal concept of what excellence looks and feels like.
- Supports striving for goals that are innovative and demanding.
- Continually seeks to identify and overcome barriers to excellent performance.
- Actively seeks to be aware of and measure oneself against best practice.

9. Having a flexible approach

- Adapts skills, pace and tone to reflect the needs of others.
- Shows sensitivity to the needs and emotions of others.
- Respects the values, attitudes and beliefs of others.
- Employs all aspects of personal competence – intuitive, intellectual, emotional – to challenge inflexibility.
- Suspends judgement and contemplates the unthinkable.

10. Thinking and understanding

- Focuses on facts, issues outcomes when handling an emotional situation.
- Balances logic with intuition/emotional intelligence.
- Reconciles and employs a variety of perspectives when trying to make sense of a situation.

Analysing

- Identifies a range of elements in a situation.
- Breaks down processes into tasks and activities.
- Finds a number of perspectives on a problem.
- Identifies the implications, consequences or cause-and-effect relationships in a situation.

Conceptualising

- Helps build a complete and valid picture from a restricted or incomplete picture.
- Draws on own experience and evidence from other sources to identify problems and understand context.
- Identifies patterns or meaning from events and data not obviously connected.

The Scottish Credit and Qualifications Framework

The Scottish Credit and Qualifications Framework (SCQF) is a way of understanding and comparing qualifications in Scotland. Its main purposes are to:

- make the relationships between the various qualifications that are available clearer;
- make the progression and transfer between qualifications easier by clarifying entry and exit points and routes for progression.

Further information is available from *www.scqf.org.uk*.

SCQF Level	SQA National Units/Courses	Higher Education	Scottish Vocational Qualification	SCQF Level
12		Doctorate		12
11		Masters	SVQ 5	11
10		Honours degree		10
9		Ordinary degree		9
8		HND/Dip HE	SVQ 4	8
7	Advanced Higher	HNC/Cert HE		7

SCQF Level	SQA National Units/Courses	Higher Education	Scottish Vocational Qualification	SCQF Level
6	Higher		SVQ 3	6
5	Intermediate 2/ Credit S Grade		SVQ 2	5
4	Intermediate 1/ General S Grade		SVQ 1	4
3	Access 3/ Foundation S Grade			3
2	Access 2			2
1	Access 1			1

Cross-referencing of text with ILM qualifications

Level 3

G1 Coaching skills and standards

		Topic	*Pages*
G1.1	Good practice in coaching	The preparation of the coach and coaching contract	63, 68
G1.2	Learning styles and barriers to effective coaching	Understanding practical learning styles	45
G1.3	Evaluate and plan the use of resources	Planning a coaching intervention or programme	14
G1.4	Communication skills in coaching	Listening, questioning and the catalytic toolkit	23, 32, 50
G1.5	Record and assess learning	Supervision and CPD	203

G2 The coaching process

		Topic	Pages
G2.1	Agree learning goals for coaching	The coaching contract and action planning	68, 175
G2.2	Plan a coaching programme	Planning a coaching intervention or programme	14
G2.3	Undertake coaching in the workplace	All of Chapters 2, 3 and 4	

Level 4

H1 Developing performance through coaching and mentoring

		Topic	Pages
H1.1	Good practice in coaching and mentoring	The preparation of the coach and coaching contract	63, 68
H1.2	Values and standards in coaching and mentoring	Ethics in coaching	158
H1.3	Building relationships and commitment	Developing relationships and the four pillars of trust	75, 86

H1 Developing performance through coaching and mentoring cont.

		Topic	Pages
H1.4	Develop questioning and listening skills	Listening, questioning and the catalytic toolkit	23, 32, 50
H1.5	Organisational implications of coaching and mentoring	Team coaching, coaching evaluation and bottom line benifits	146, 191, 198

H2 Coaching and mentoring practice

		Topic	Pages
H2.1	Agree development goals	The coaching contract and action planning	68, 175
H2.2	Planning a coaching or mentoring programme	Planning a coaching intervention or programme	14
H2.3	Undertake coaching or mentoring and reflect on own performance	CPD and supervision	203

Level 5

J1   Developing leadership through mentoring and executive coaching

		Topic	Pages
J1.1	Understanding leadership mentoring and executive coaching	The context of coaching and definition of coaching	2, 9
J1.2	Commitment to leadership mentoring and executive coaching	All of Chapters 1, 3 and 6 plus the Conclusion	
J1.3	Develop questioning and listening skills for coaching or mentoring	All of Chapters 2 and 4	
J1.4	Ethics, values and belief systems in action	Team coaching, ethics in coaching, switching perspectives and action planning	146, 158, 167, 175
J1.5	Support the growth of leadership capability	All chapters	

J2 Leadership mentoring and executive coaching practice

		Topic	Pages
J2.1	Diagnose, reflect on and plan to develop own skills, knowledge, attitudes and beliefs	CPD and supervision	203
J2.2	Engage actively in peer mentoring and coaching	CPD and supervision	203
J2.3	Undertake mentoring or coaching and reflect on own performance	Chapters 3 and 4, CPD and supervision	203

Bibliography

Agazarian, Y. and Peters, R. (1995) *The Visible and Invisible Group*. Karnac Books.

Alfred, G., Garvey, R. and Smith, R. (1998) *The Mentoring Pocketbook*. Management Pocketbooks.

Argyris, C. and Schön, D. (1992) *Theory in Practice: Increasing Professional Effectiveness*. Jossey-Bass Wiley.

Arriens, Angeles (1993) *The Four-Fold Way: Walking the Paths of the Warrior, Teacher, Healer, and Visionary*. HarperSanFrancisco.

Bee, Roland and Bee, Frances (1998) *Constructive Feedback*. Chartered Institute of Personnel & Development.

Berne, Eric (1970) *Games People Play*. Penguin Books.

Biech, Elaine (1998) *The Business of Consulting*. Pfeiffer Wiley.

Binney, G. and Williams, C. (1995) *Leaning into the Future*. Nicholas Brealey.

Bion, W. (1990) *Experiences in Group*. Routledge.

Blanchard, K., Lacinak, T., Tompkins, C. and Ballard, J (2003) *Whale Done!* Nicholas Brealey.

Blanchard, Ken (1987) *Leadership and the One Minute Leader*. HarperCollins.

Block, P. (1996) *Stewardship – Choosing Service Over Self-Interest*. Berret-Koehler.

Block, P. (2000) *Flawless Consulting – A Guide to Getting Your Expertise Used*. Pfeiffer Wiley.

Bolchover, D. and Brady, C. (2002) *The 90-Minute Manager*. Financial Times Prentice Hall.

Bridges, W. (1995) *Managing Transitions: Making the Most of Change*. Nicholas Brealey.

Buzan, Tony (1989) *Use Your Head*. BBC.

Cockman, P., Evans, W. and Reynolds, P. (1998) *Consulting for Real People*. McGraw-Hill Education Europe.

Coleman, D. (1996) *Emotional Intelligence*. Bloomsbury.

Cooper, Robert and Sawaf, Ayman (1996) *Executive EQ – Emotional Intelligence in Business*. Texere Publishing.

Covey, S. (2004) *The Seven Habits of Highly Effective People*. Simon & Schuster.

Covey, S.R. and Merrill, A.R. (1997) *First Things First*. Simon & Schuster.

Csikszentmihalyi, M. (1992) *Flow – The Psychology of Happiness*. Rider.

Cunninghm, Ian and Dawes, Graham (1998) *Exercises for Developing Coaching Capability*. CIPD.

Downey, Myles (1999) *Effective Coaching*. Texere Publishing.

Drucker, Peter, (1994) *Post-Capitalist Society*. Butterworth-Heinemann.

Dryden, G. and Vos, J. (1994) *The Learning Revolution*. Accelerated Learning Systems.

Duff, A. (2003) *Gentleness*. Xlibris.

Eaton, J. and Johnson, R. (2000) *Coaching Successfully*. Dorling Kindersley.

Eriksson, Sven-Goran and Railo, Willi (2002) *Making Lions Roar* (DVD). International Licensing and Copyright Ltd.

Eysenck, M. and Keane, M. (2000) *Cognitive Psychology.* Psychology Press.

Ferrucci, Piero (1993) *What We May Be.* HarperCollins.

Fisher, R. and Ury, W. (1997) *Getting to Yes – Negotiating Agreement Without Giving In.* Arrow.

Flaherty, J. (1999) *Coaching – Evoking Excellence in Others.* Butterworth-Heinemann.

Flavell, J., Miller, P. and Miller, S. (1993) *Cognitive Development.* Prentice Hall.

Fleming, I. (1998) *The Coaching Pocketbook.* Management Pocketbooks.

Fournies, Ferdinand (1999) *Coaching for Improved Performance.* McGraw-Hill Education.

Gallwey, Tim (1986) *The Inner Game of Tennis.* Pan.

Gallwey, Tim (2002) *The Inner Game of Work.* Texere Publishing.

Goldberg, Marilee (1997) *The Art of the Question: A Guide to Short-Term Question-Centered Therapy.* Wiley.

Goldsmith, M. and Lyons, L. (2000) *Coaching for Leadership.* Jossey-Bass Wiley.

Goss, Tracy (1996) *The Last Word on Power.* Piatkus Books.

Hale, Judith (1998) *The Performance Consultants Fieldbook.* Pfeiffer Wiley.

Handy, Charles (1995) *The Age of Paradox.* Harvard Business School Press.

Handy, Charles (1995) *The Age of Unreason.* Random House Business Books.

Handy, Charles (2001) *Understanding Organizations.* Arrow.

Hargrove, Robert (1995) *Masterful Coaching.* Pfeiffer Wiley.

Heaney, Seamus (1999) *Beowulf.* Faber & Faber.

Heron, John (1990) *Helping the Client – A Creative Practical Guide.* Sage.

Heron, John (1999) *The Complete Facilitator's Handbook,* 2nd edn. Kogan Page.

Hirschhorn, L. (1990) *Managing in the New Team Environment.* Addison-Wesley.

Hirschhorn, L. (1990) *The Workplace Within – Psychodynamics of Organizational Life.* MIT Press.

Husdson, Frederic (1999) *The Handbook of Coaching.* Jossey-Bass Wiley.

Jackson, P. and Delehanty, H. (1996) *Sacred Hoops.* Hyperion Books.

Jacobs, M. (1999) *Psychodynamic Counselling in Action.* Sage.

John, E. and Johnson, R. (2000) *Coaching Successfully.* Dorling Kindersley.

Kaplan, H. and Sadock, B. (1993) *Comprehensive Group Psychotherapy.* Lippincott Williams & Wilkins.

Katzenbach, Jon R. and Smith, Douglas K. *Wisdom of Teams: Creating the High-Performance Organization.* HarperBusiness.

Kearns, P. and Miller, T. (1997) *Measuring the Impact of Training and Development on the Bottom Line.* Financial Times Prentice Hall.

Kelleher, Herb (2002) *The Art of Coaching in Business*, 2nd edn (Video). Greylock Associates.

Kinlaw, Dennis (1993) *Coaching for Commitment*. Pfeiffer Wiley.

Kinlaw, Dennis (1997) *Coaching – Winning Strategies for Individuals and Teams*. Gower.

Knight, Sue (2002) *NLP at Work*. Nicholas Brealey.

Kubler-Ross, Elisabeth (1993) *On Children and Death*. Collier Paperbacks.

Landsberg, Max (1997) *The Tao of Coaching*. HarperCollins Business.

Landsberg, Max (1999) *The Tao of Motivation*. HarperCollins Business.

Lawley, J. and Tompkins, P. (2000) *Metaphors in Mind*. Developing Company Press.

Legend of Bagger Vance, The (2000) 20th Century Fox (DVD).

Lucas, Robert (1994) *Coaching Skills – A Guide for Supervisors*. Irwin Professional.

Matson, H. and Reilo, W. (2001) *Sven-Goran Eriksson on Football*. Carlton Books.

McLeod, Angus (2003) *Performance Coaching*. Crown House Publishing.

McMaster, M., Grindler, J. and Grinder, J. (1994) *Precision: New Approach to Communication*. Metamorphous Press.

Mearns, D. and Thorne, B. (1999) *Person Centred Counselling in Action*. Sage.

Miller, E. (1993) *From Dependency to Autonomy*. Free Association Books.

Millman, D. (1994) *The Inner Athlete*. Stillpoint Publishing.

Murray, Margo (2001) *Beyond the Myths and Magic of Mentoring*. Jossey-Bass Wiley.

Myss, C. (2002) *Sacred Contracts*. Bantam.

Neuland, Michele (1998) *The World of Moderation*. Neuland Publications for Active Learning.

Norretranders, T. (1999) *The User Illusion*. Penguin Books.

O'Neill, M.B. (2000) *Executive Coaching with Backbone and Heart*. Jossey-Bass Wiley.

Page, Tony (1996) *Diary of a Change Agent*. Gower.

Parkin, Margaret (1998) *Tales for Trainers*. Kogan Page.

Parkin, Margaret (2001) *Tales for Coaching*. Kogan Page.

Parsloe, E. (1999) *The Manager as a Coach and Mentor*. Chartered Institute of Personnel & Development.

Parsloe, Eric (1995) *Coaching, Mentoring and Assessing*. Kogan Page.

Parsloe, Eric and Wray, M. (2000) *Coaching and Mentoring – Practical Methods to Improve Learning*. Kogan Page.

Peltier, B. (2001) *The Psychology of Executive Coaching*. Brunner-Routledge.

Pilger, John (2003) *New Rulers of the World*. Verso.

Reddy, Brendan (1995) *Intervention Skills*. Pfeiffer Wiley.

Robinson, D. and Robinson, J. (1996) *Performance Consulting*. Berrett-Koehler.

Rogers, Carl (1995a) *Client Centered Therapy*. Trans-Atlantic Publications.

Rogers, Carl (1995b) *On Becoming a Person*. Mariner Books.

Salisbury, F., Neary, C. and O'Conner, K. (2001) *Coaching Champions*. Oak Tree Press.

Scott Peck, M. (1988) *The Road Less Travelled*. Rider.

Scott Peck, M. (1990) *The Different Drum: Community Making and Peace.* Arrow.

Secretan, Lance (1998) *Reclaiming Higher Ground.* McGraw-Hill Education.

Senge, Peter (1993) *The Fifth Discipline – The Art of the Learning Organization.* Random House Business Books.

Shafir, R. (2000) *The Zen of Listening.* Quest Books.

Shaw, Nadir and Walton, A. (1994) *Discontinuous Change.* Jossey-Bass Wiley.

Silberman, Mel (1998) *Active Training.* Pfeiffer Wiley.

Skiffington, S. and Zeus, P. (2000) *The Complete Guide to Coaching at Work.* McGraw-Hill Education.

Stevens, A. (2001) *Jung: A Very Short Introduction.* Oxford Paperbacks.

Stewart, I. and Joines, V. (1987) *TA Today.* Lifespace Publishing.

Stimson, N. (1994) *Coaching Your Employees.* Kogan Page.

Storr, A. (2001) *Freud: A Very Short Introduction.* Oxford Paperbacks.

Tamkin, P., Yarnell, J. and Kerrin, M. (2002) *Kirkpatrick and Beyond*, Institute for Employment Studies Report No. 392. Available from *http://www.employment-studies.co.uk*.

Tannen, Deborah (1994) *Talking from 9 to 5: Women and Men at Work.* Quill.

Tice, Lou (1997) *Personal Coaching for Results.* STL.

Trevino, Linda K. and Nelson, Katherine A. (1995) *Managing Business Ethics.* John Wiley & Sons.

Truss, Lynn (2004) *Eats, Shoots and Leaves.* Gotham Books.

Vella, Jane (2000) *Taking Learning to Task*. Jossey-Bass Wiley.

Voss, Tony (1996) *Sharpen Your Team Skills in Coaching*. McGraw-Hill Education Europe.

Watkins, M.J. and Gardiner, J.M. (1979) 'An appreciation of the generate-recognise theory of recall', *Journal of Learning and Verbal Behaviour*, 18, 687–704.

Weisbord, M. (1991) *Productive Workplaces*. Jossey-Bass Wiley.

Weisbord, M.R. (1993) *Discovering Common Ground*. Berrett Publishers.

Weisbord, M. and Janoff, S. (1995) *Future Search*. Berrett-Koehler.

Westcott, L. and Landau, J. (1996) *A Picture's Worth a Thousand Words*. Pfeiffer Wiley.

Wheatley, M.J. (1994) *Leadership and the New Science*. Berrett-Koehler.

Whitmore, Sir John (1996) *Coaching for Performance – Growing People, Performance and Purpose*. Nicholas Brealey.

Whitmore, Sir John (1997) *Need, Greed or Freedom*. Element Books.

Whittaker, Mike and Cartwright, Anne (1997) *32 Activities on Coaching and Mentoring*. Gower.

Whyte, David (1994) *The Heart Aroused*. Bantam Doubleday Dell.

Whyte, David (2001) *Crossing the Unknown Sea*. Michael Joseph.

Wilber, K. (1996) *A Brief History of Everything*. Michelle Anderson Publishing.

Wragg, E.C. and Brown, G. (2001) *Questioning in the Secondary School*. RoutledgeFalmer.

Zachary, Lois and Daloz, L.A. (2000) *The Mentor's Guide*. Jossey-Bass Wiley.

Zeus, P. and Skiffington, S. (2003) *The Coaching at Work Toolkit*. McGraw-Hill Education.

Index

return on investment (ROI), 193
Rogers, Carl, 23, 28, 49
Rogers, Keith, 46
rule of three, 186, 187

sample questions:
  assumptions, 38
  consequences, 37
  histories, 37
Sawaf, Ayman, 172
Schön, D., 21
SCQF, 235
selective echoing, 55
Shafir, Rebecca Z., 60
simple echoing, 54
Skiffington, S., 2, 3, 174
skill/will matrix, 107, 108, 112,
  215
  application, 109
small team audit, 149
Smith, Douglas K., 146, 155
Smith, Will, 79
STOP tool, 112, 114–17, 167
  uses, 119–20
strategic questions, 39
  first level, 40
  second level, 40
  third level, 41
success criteria, 191
suggestion map, 102, 104, 106
summarising, 103
supervision, 203
  qualities, 206
surface processor, 49
switching perspectives, 167, 171
symbolic domain of experience,
  135
symbolic meaning, 139

Tannen, Deborah, 23, 28
team:

basics, 147
coaching, 146
leader, 152
performance curve, 150
technique of reflection, 26
therapeutic:
  effect, 206
  process, 142–5
thinker, 47, 48
three D-model, 182, 185
Tidswell, Karen, 49
Tompkins, Penny, 133, 135, 201
traditional approach, 10
training, 13
transformational coaching, 10
transitional coaching, 10
travel path, 169
Trevino, Linda K., 174
triangulation approach, 200
two-stage theory, 186

verbal metaphors, 138
verbaliser, 47, 48
visualiser, 47, 48

Wagoner, David, 64
Wallaczek, Miki, 5
Watkins, 186
way forward, 97
Welsh, Anne, 207
Whitmore, John (Sir), 5, 19, 97,
  100, 126, 173
Whyte, David, 5, 52, 64, 90
Willis, Pauline, 162, 205
working group, 151
wrap-up, 97
Wray, Monica, 129

Yarnell, J., 201

Zeus, P., 2, 3, 174